Lonely Trails
around
Lakeland

LONELY TRAILS
around
LAKELAND

by

Graham K. Dugdale

Illustrations by David Macaulay

Westmorland Gazette, Kendal, Cumbria

© **Westmorland Gazette, 1994**

ISBN 0 902272 92 6

Published by
Westmorland Gazette
22 Stricklandgate, Kendal, Cumbria LA9 4NE

Printed by
The Craven Herald & Pioneer
Skipton, North Yorkshire

THE TRAILS

As with the previous books in this series, there is a noticeable bias in favour of the eastern sector of Lakeland, in addition to including that most spicy western fringe of the Yorkshire Dales. I have decided to adopt a reverse ordering of the walks, beginning with the easiest and finishing with the most strenuous. Why? This would appear to be the most positive way to encourage couch potatoes to switch off the box and do a little more exercise than walking upstairs to bed. The listing is of course arbitrary and my own personal view. If anybody chances to agree, it will most definitely be a first and as such worthy of a pub lunch anyday. But don't forget to bring your cheque book.

Having returned to fells not visited since the opening volume, it has become clear that features can change rapidly. Cairns come and go. Walls are replaced by fences. Trees grow and are cut down (especially conifers). Only the mountains themselves remain untainted by the hand of Man. The walks are as described when I did them. Any false trails or red herrings that have appeared since should not, therefore, be laid at my door.

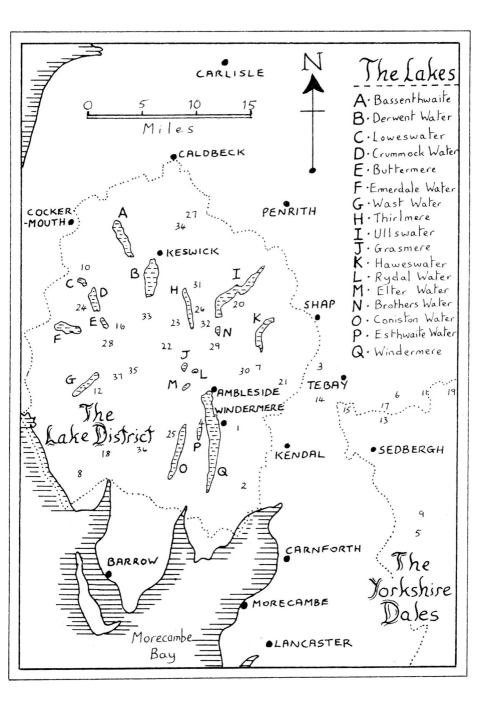

N

The Lakes

A · Bassenthwaite
B · Derwent Water
C · Loweswater
D · Crummock Water
E · Buttermere
F · Ennerdale Water
G · Wast Water
H · Thirlmere
I · Ullswater
J · Grasmere
K · Haweswater
L · Rydal Water
M · Elter Water
N · Brothers Water
O · Coniston Water
P · Esthwaite Water
Q · Windermere

CARLISLE

0   5   10   15
Miles

CALDBECK

COCKER-MOUTH

A

27
34

PENRITH

KESWICK

B
C
D
E
F

10

24

33

H
J
M
G

31
26
23   32
22   29
37 35
12

I

20

K
N

L
30 7

SHAP

3

TEBAY

14

6   11   19
15   17
13

The Lake District

AMBLESIDE
WINDERMERE

21

SEDBERGH

25

P
O

4
Q

1

2

KENDAL

18   36
8

9
5

BARROW

CARNFORTH

MORECAMBE

The Yorkshire Dales

Morecambe Bay

LANCASTER

INTRODUCTION

Having spent much of my adult life wandering across the fell country of northern England, it never ceases to amaze me how very fortunate I am to have been granted the privileged status of resident.

A chance encounter with a *Gazette* editor saw the start of my glittering career as a Lakeland guide, which led to the publication of *Remote Walks*. The follow-up, *Hikes,* was a compilation of walks of a more strenuous nature. Involvement with the *Around Lakeland* guides has made it evident that one can spend a lifetime fell walking without finding it necessary to repeat circuits. We all too have favourite walks to be revisited at irregular intervals, each time from a novel direction, thus providing a new perspective from which to enjoy afresh the solitude of the fells.

Such then was my realisation over many years that walks in and around the District are many and varied. And herein lies the motivation for this third in the series. It is difficult to avoid duplication or repitition in such a compact area, but this has been kept to a minimum. *Lonely Trails* must, therefore, be the final contribution to a series of walks catering for those hardy souls who relish their own company in territory far from the well-trodden highways.

Once again, a summit cairn remains the principal objective of each walk. Valley trails possess their own intrinsic magnetism, but this is rambling, and every true fellwanderer would be forever casting an envious eye towards the heights above.

A famous son of Lakeland, now resident atop his venerated Haystacks, regarded the contributions he made to the sport of fellcraft as a series of love letters devoted to the hills that gave him so much pleasure. My own humble offerings reflect a similar sentiment. Ever since that first winter scramble up Red Screes clad in a torn Pakamac and ribbed wellies at the tender age of thirteen, the hynotic aura of the fells has been a part of my very being. Perhaps like the inimitable AW, the spell will only be broken when the Grim Reaper snaps his icy fingers.

This volume might well be the finale, but my boots have many miles left in them yet. I have in mind the desire to walk the Lake District National Park boundary keeping to rights of way as much as possible — a long distance walk

6

round the outer rim and, in consequence, more an extended ramble rather than a fell walk. Perchance if the publishers can be persuaded you will be able to follow me in years to come. That would truly be a remote walk around Lakeland on lonely trails.

Until then, Happy Hiking!

Graham K. Dugdale

BY THE SAME AUTHOR

Guide Books
Remote Walks around Lakeland
Hikes around Lakeland

Novel
High Plains Vendetta. Robert Hale Ltd.

ACKNOWLEDGMENTS

W. Rollinson: *A History of Man in the Lake District.* J. M. Dent & Sons Ltd.
R. Millward & A. Robinson: *The Lake District.* Eyre Methuen
W. Rollinson (Editor): *The Lake District, Landscape Heritage.* David & Charles
Lakescene Magazine for their encouragement and sponsorship

KEY TO MAPS

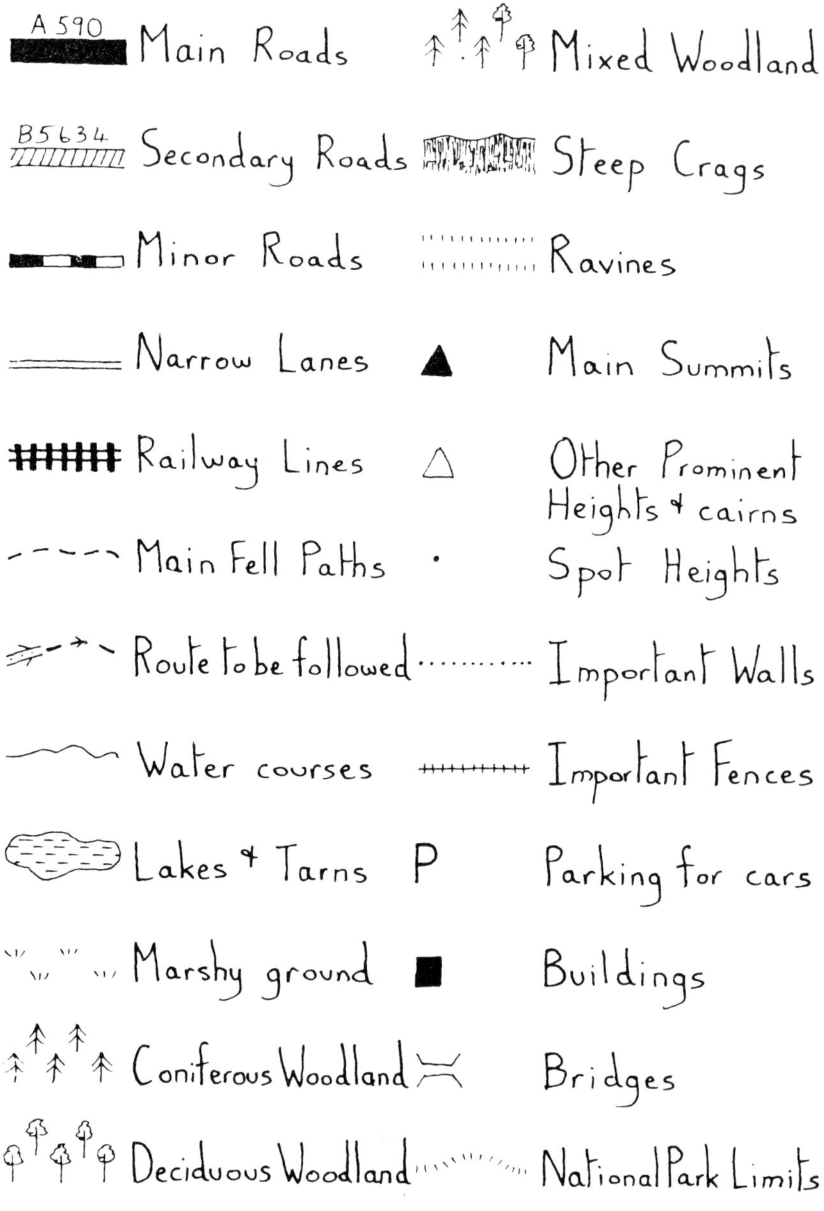

A590 Main Roads

B5634 Secondary Roads

Minor Roads

Narrow Lanes

Railway Lines

- - - - Main Fell Paths

→ - → Route to be followed

Water courses

Lakes & Tarns

Marshy ground

Coniferous Woodland

Deciduous Woodland

Mixed Woodland

Steep Crags

Ravines

▲ Main Summits

△ Other Prominent Heights & cairns

· Spot Heights

·········· Important Walls

+++++++ Important Fences

P Parking for cars

■ Buildings

Bridges

National Park Limits

1. WINDERMERE'S OTHER HIGH SCHOOL

Start and Finish: Dropping down into Windermere from Kendal, there is a lay-by on the right of the A591 immediately opposite the start of this walk.

Summit Climbed: School Knot — 760 feet

Total Height Climbed: 400 feet

Distance Walked: 5½ miles

Nearest Centre: Windermere

Map Required: Ordnance Survey English Lakes 1:25000, South East area sheet

INTRODUCTION

One could be forgiven for ignoring the low cluster of hills to the east of Windermere when approaching from Kendal. All eyes will doubtless be focussed on the rugged skyline ahead. But when the mist obscures everything above 1000 feet, these lower fells assume a greater significance in the pecking order. School Knott is the most prominent blip on this gently undulating landscape, if not the highest, that dubious honour being granted to its neighbour, Grandsire.

Unlike any other hill in the locality, School Knott can be legally trodden by means of a public right-of-way. The access path below the northern boundary wall has, however, recently (August 1993) been officially relocated one field to the north. If you intend to make full use of my map (a wise decision), no problems should be encountered. Ignore the 295 metres (exact) of path illustrated on current Ordnance Survey maps starting at GR 420976.

9

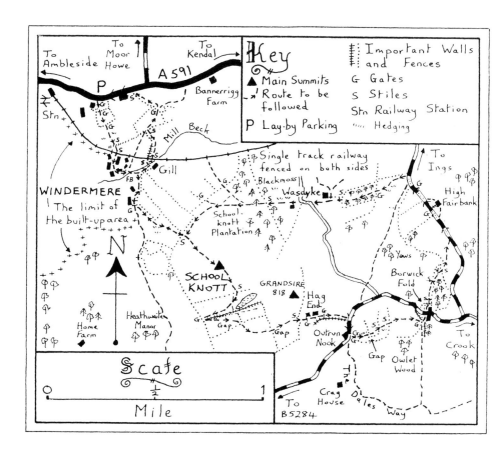

Well known to the residents of Windermere, one is unlikely to bump into anybody other than farmers beyond School Knott, except perhaps recalcitrant cattle.

For those who have driven far, but still feel the need to get their new boots dirty, here is a late afternoon stroll across sublime acres of pastoral tranquillity that are as much Lakeland as any Striding Edge or Jack's Rake. Ease into the feel of the Lake District by treading little known trails that are a delight to follow. After all, Helvellyn will still be there tomorrow.

A small slice of the walk between Schoolknott Tarn and Hag End takes in the Dales Way. Designated as a long distance footpath in 1968, it meanders for 84 miles between Bowness and Ilkley across two National Parks. Okay for next Sunday?

ROUTE DESCRIPTION

Cross the A591 and pass through a small gate left of a farm. Another gate gives onto a field. Follow the wall to yet a third gate after which, slant left across a rather boggy tract. Hidden in a hedge close to the railway is an old iron kissing-gate. Twenty yards to the east, access to the single-line track bound for Windermere is gained up an embankment. Stop, look and listen!

Beyond the railway, we enter the outer Windermere suburb of Heath-waite. A stroll along Ghyll Road and straight across Mill Rise brings us into a narrow hedged lane. Cross Mill Beck bridge taking the right fork signposted to School Knott. The lane passes behind a group of houses.

Immediately after a gate/stile, join the new path branching left alongside a wall and climbing steadily to the boundary wall stile. A lightweight grass trod meanders up to the highest point, a super view west across Windermere, but strangely lacking the obligatory summit cairn.

Cruise down the opposite slope aiming for the fishing tarn — no poachers please. Swing right, away from the placid waters heading south west, to meet the Dales Way, which cuts back east through a gate. Cross the rough-cast field pasture through a gap in the wall following a course bearing left and another gap before arriving at Hag End.

11

Climb over the stile, ambling past a generation of defunct Land Rovers, now a sanctuary for nesting hens. Two gates and down the farm access road brings us to an open fell road. Head right, coming to a halt at Outrun Nook road gate. Beyond and immediately left is a further gate pointing the way east along a hedge and through a gap. Keep the wall on your right for 100 yards, then fork away to locate the wall stile. Slant half left across a bed of reedy sponge to another stile, and then maintain an easterly course to Borwick Fold.

Make a left through two gates past the farm buildings to emerge on the metalled road again. Turn right then left alongside an old garage. Cross a somewhat overgrown stile, passing a garden pond and over another concealed on the right. Continue along the left side of a wood up to a kink in the wall. Once over the stile, aim for the far side of the wood, after which a brief descent, veering north away from the wood, brings us to the road yet again.

Walk down the road towards Ings past the farm of High Fairbank set back. A hundred yards beyond the second road gate, head left alongside a wall towards a small wood having a gate at either side. Keep west after Whasdike to join a metalled farm access road. When this swings sharp right, continue ahead past a small water hut pursuing a direct course for Schoolknott Plantation. Enter this wood via a wall stile.

Carry on through the thinning tree cover, ignoring deviations from a straight course, until a wall is approached after which we bear left alongside. Upon reaching the wall stile below School Knott, retrace your steps back to the fork in the road abutting the new housing estate. Press ahead towards Gill, branching left across Mill Beck then immediately right along a fence to the railway.

Once again, stop, look and listen! Encouraging train drivers to practise their emergency stop routine is not to be recommended. Follow the fence on the opposite side, swinging left along a wall. Beyond a stile, join a substantial track to head right. At the far side of the field, choose the gate on the right. Deviation from a direct course at this point could be a 'shocking' experience.

At the main road, take a left back towards the town and lay-by, and the conclusion of an unusual walk over terrain largely unknown to non-residents. Care is needed along footways that are often rarely trod. But nevertheless, it provides a stimulating taster prior to any loftier challenges being attempted.

2. WOODED WHITBARROW

Start and Finish: A roadside pull-in on the A5074 Lyth Valley road immediately south west of the entrance to The High Farm at grid reference 442904.

Summit Climbed: Lord's Seat   — 706 feet

Total Height Climbed: 600 feet

Distance Walked: 6 miles

Nearest Centre: Brigsteer

Maps Required: Ordnance Survey English Lakes 1:25000, South East area sheet, plus Ordnance Survey Pathfinder Series 1:25000, Milnthorpe SD 48/58 sheet

INTRODUCTION

Most visitors to Lakeland race up the M6 motorway driving straight in by way of the main A591 road, a route that becomes increasingly busy as spring turns into summer. Few have any notion of the de-luxe approach to Windermere through the Lyth Valley gained by a short detour across the estuary of the River Kent. Watch for the Windermere turn off as the mighty rampart of Whitbarrow is neared close to the old hamlet clustered around Gilpin Bridge.

The wooded slopes on the left flank of the valley once extended unbroken to the shores of Lake Windermere and were home to the now extinct wild boar. In days of yore, one such ferocious specimen roamed the district wreaking havoc amongst the lowland settlers. It was only due to the gallant bravery of one, Richard de Gylpin, who tracked the savage beast to his secret lair, that it was eventually despatched to the happy hunting grounds.

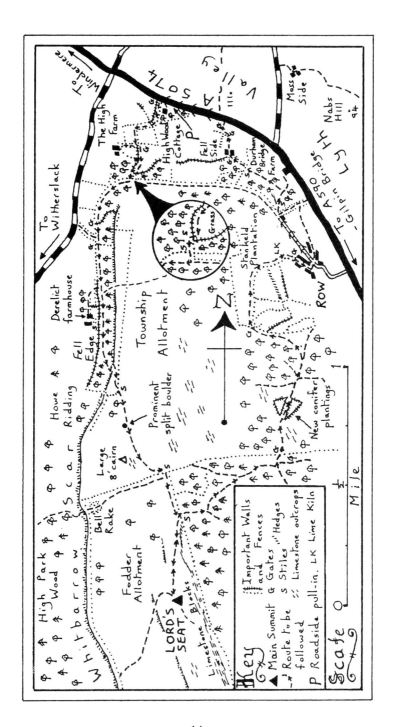

Key

✕ Main Summit G Gates S Stiles
▲ Route to be followed
P Roadside pull-in. LK Lime Kiln

⋮⋮ Important Walls and Fences
⋯⋯ 'ʼʼ Hedges
⊰⊰ Limestone outcrops

Scale 0   ½   1 Mile

Today the valley is renowned for its damson blossom, the exuberant display of white petals giving the appearance of a rogue snowfall in May. Fruit lovers should reserve their visit for mid-September when the damson crop is being harvested. Whitbarrow's wooded limestone bulk provides a welcome screen to shelter the fruit-bearing trees from storms blasting in from the west. Limestone is said to imbue a certain sweetness to the soil, which has helped to establish the Lyth Valley as a very special place for damson growth in Britain. In the past, some farms have been known to produce over 50 tons of fruit in a season, although these days they would be lucky indeed to reach five in view of declining tree regeneration.

This, therefore, is the connoisseur's route entering South Lakeland by the back door, a truly memorable sojourn along a splendidly tranquil valley. The drive north along the west side of the valley sets the scene for an easy-going wander amidst impressive limestone woodland.

ROUTE DESCRIPTION

From the pull-in, walk north for 50 yards taking the first right along the High Farm access road. After a sharp zig-zag, when the walled approach to the farm buildings is reached, bear left through a gate then immediately right to follow a fence uphill to the corner of a small wood. Keep to the outer edge of the trees to the top corner. Cross the stile into the copse. No more than ten yards uphill, a wall stile gives onto a major track circling the northern limit of Whitbarrow's limestone upthrust.

Turn right along the track, swinging round to the western side along a pleasant level sward that follows the lower edge of the Scar. Heading due south, the tree cover on this increasingly steep flank becomes ever more pronounced, soon merging into a sylvan tunnel between two gates. Once more into the open, we approach the farmstead of Fell Edge, the house now merely a ruined shell in contrast to the well-maintained adjacent barns.

Soon after, the narrow path veers away from the accompanying fence to begin a gentle ascent of the roughly wooded escarpment. Immediately beyond a sharply defined dogleg, the path emerges from the wooded screen onto the plateau. Keep right, aiming for the wall corner, there to mount a stile and head north west towards a prominent boulder on the near horizon. At this point, our objective hoves into view a mile to the north.

Continue across the open grass tract, keeping left of a well-built cairn and forking in to join a substantial wall crossing the fell. Follow it in an easterly direction until a gate and stile are reached allowing access to the Hervey Nature Reserve. Run by the Cumbria Wildlife Trust, it is one of 13 such designated areas set up locally, being a haven for breeding birds in addition to red and roe deer, which can often be seen in the lower woods. Ash, juniper and birch are the natural flora, overshadowed by extensive conifer planting especially on Farrer's Allotment at Whitbarrow's southern extremity.

Beyond the stile, head south along a wall until the path is forced away and up towards the summit by a low limestone scarp. The eastern prospect from Lord's Seat is severely restricted by tree coverage. And that to the west gives no indication of the savage cliffs of raw limestone crag standing guard along Witherslack's hidden valley. Woven into the large monument is a plaque to the gentleman who first set up the nature reserve and who died in 1967 at the age of 74 years.

Retrace your steps back to the wall and watch for a stile, which leads you into the confines of the woods. After 150 yards, take a left down a stony trail breaking from the main track. Keep downhill as far as a T-junction where you should turn left carrying straight on to reach a wall. Pass through a small gate into Township Plantation and down a narrow way between two recently fenced off conifer plantings. At a crossroads, go straight over on a much thinner trail, which makes a wide sweep to the left slanting in towards a wall at the edge of the woods.

A gate gives onto a large open field. Accompany the wall in a wide arc to the right to the tiny hamlet of Row. Pass through a gate and down a short rough street between renovated farm buildings, and turn sharp left into a metalled lane heading north west for a quarter of a mile. When a dirt lane veers right at a cottage, enter Durham Bridge Wood via a stile and follow the rutted track until a clear left deviates from this. Becoming ever more indistinct, it leads us to a wall stile beyond which it is necessary to adopt various ungainly postures to negotiate fallen trees and hidden boulders on the steep descent of this northern rim of the Scar. Two gates at the bottom adjacent to an old caravan give access to the farmyard of Fell Side.

Exit at the far side, watching for a right fork off this main access road, which takes us through a hedged gap. This old right of way swings right to join the Lyth Valley road a quarter of a mile east of our roadside pull-in. This little-known corner of the National Park contrasts markedly with the glacial peaks and troughs normally associated with Lakeland but is no less attractive for that.

3. BIRKBECK SANDWICH

Start and Finish: Ample parking space is available on the open grass verge at the hamlet of Scout Green (GR 593077), which lies three miles west of Orton close to the M6 motorway and main railway line.

Summit Climbed:	Crag Hill	— 1300 feet
Total Height Climbed:	700 feet	
Distance Walked:	7 miles	
Nearest Centre:	Orton	
Map Required:	Ordnance Survey English Lakes 1:25000, South East area sheet	

INTRODUCTION

Five miles north of Kendal, the eastern boundary of the Lake District follows the line of the A6. Just beyond Shap Summit (1385 feet), the highest point of this once major route to Scotland, a broad tract of moorland to the east provides easy walking of the highest quality. This gently shelving swell rises but little above the surrounding countryside and is more akin to Pennine than Lakeland landscape.

Unhindered by walls or fences encircling the Common, Birkbeck Fells are a delight to walk, the turf being well cropped by sheep and a wandering clutch of indigenous fell ponies. Squeezed by the high-speed rail and motorway links to the east, this common upland provides a delicious sandwich filler. Ignored and alone, it remains untouched by the hand of Man, save for the contro-versial pursuit of grouse across the north-west heather-backed slopes. The rest is all grass. The close proximity of major highways has, however, encouraged

18

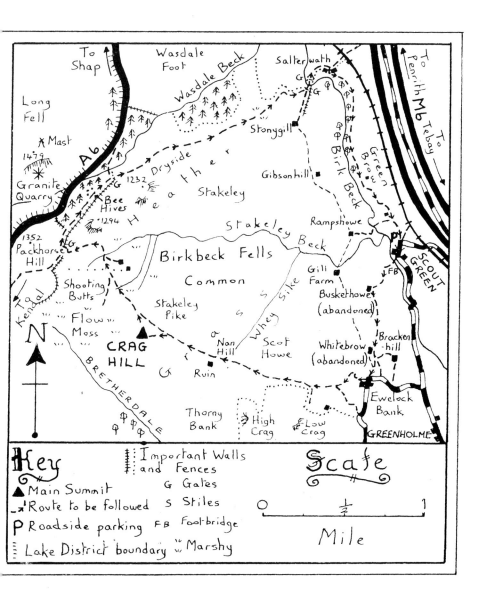

To
Shap

Wasdale
Foot

Wasdale Beck

Salterwath

To
Penrith M6 Tebay

Long
Fell

Wasdale Beck

G

G

Stonygill

A6

✳ Mast

1479

Dryside

t h e r

Gibsonhill

Birk Beck

Green Brow

Granite
Quarry

G 1232

Bee
Hives

a

e

Stakeley

1294 H

Stakeley Beck

Rampshowe

1352
Packhorse
Hill

G

Birkbeck Fells

Common

Gill
Farm

SCOUT
GREEN

FB

Shooting
Butts

Stakeley
Pike

S

Whey Sike

Buskethowe
(abandoned)

To Kendal

Flow
Moss

S

Scot
Howe

Bracken
-hill

N

CRAG
HILL

Nan
Hill

Whitebrow
(abandoned)

G

Ruin

BRETHERDALE

Thorny
Bank

High
Crag

Flow
Crag

Ewelock
Bank

GREENHOLME

Key

Important Walls
and Fences

G Gates

Main Summit

Route to be followed

P Roadside parking

Lake District boundary

S Stiles

FB Foot-bridge

Marshy

Scale

0   ½   1

Mile

many birds to find sanctuary elsewhere judging by the decaying nature of the shooting butts.

Road and rail were designed specifically for rapid throughput of traffic and take no account of local needs. In consequence, a considerable detour along narrow lanes is necessary to set foot in the Birk Beck Valley. It, therefore, remains an isolated backwater in which numerous farms have been abandoned, yet is situated closer to modern trappings of civilisation than any other area visited in the north-west fell country.

ROUTE DESCRIPTION

Walk south across the cattle grid and past the farm buildings that make up the hamlet of Scout Green. At the far side, fork right off the road to cross Birk Beck via a footbridge. Make use of the enlarged map below to assist you in reaching Ewelock Bank without getting lost along the pathless right of way.

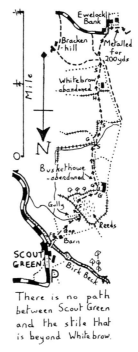

There is no path between Scout Green and the stile that is beyond Whitebrow.

20

Pass to the left of a barn ahead and cross the field, mounting the rise alongside a stream-cut gulley. At its head, bear left to cross a stile in the fence, and then head south west over a reedy pasture to the Buskethowe. The first of two abandoned farms, it still remains intact having so far resisted the onslaught of time and the elements, which indicates it cannot have been empty for long. The stile has been blocked off, so make use of the two farmyard gates to continue.

At the south-west corner of the next field where a stream crosses, gain the right side of the old wall and fence as best you can. Once again, limited usage has led to the right of passage being difficult to determine. Cross the stream and follow the fence half right to a wall stile. Thereafter, head south past the second old farm, Whitebrow, to another wall stile at the far side of the field.

Various tracks converge at this point. Continue south, bearing right to reach the sharp corner of a road close to the busy farm of Ewelock Bank. Immediately before the main buildings, take a right along an open track, metalled for the first 200 yards. It climbs steadily for half a mile before veering towards a wall on the left. Ignore all tracks forking in from the left.

A grassy groove makes a bee-line across Scot Howe, passing right of a ruin that could only have been erected for shepherds tending their flocks in the days prior to the advent of the powered quadcycle. Crag Hill, the highlight of our day, is the only blip on an otherwise rolling horizon. Leave the main route crossing trackless sheep pasture to gain the only slab of exposed rock in the vicinity, site of a prestigious if somewhat grisly cairn with a weather-beaten sheep's skull atop it.

Once the splendid isolation of this raised dais has been fully absorbed, head north towards the distant pair of shooting huts. Take advantage of a distinct sheep trod in the grass crossing the upper reaches of Stakeley Beck. It joins a wide gravel road, which should be followed to its terminus at a gate and T-junction. Turn right along the forest access road through another gate. Then head north east along the edge of a conifer plantation. Halfway along, watch for some bee hives on the left.

At the end of the wood, the road veers left over Wasdale Old Bridge to rejoin the A6. Our way lies to the right through a fence gate along a clear trail in the heather. Keep above the valley bottom, which accommodates

Wasdale Beck. Beyond the second plantation, the bridleway slants down to the in-take wall, there to accompany a minor tributary gully down to valley level alongside the wall.

A gate gives onto the farm access track to Stonygill. Make a left over the bridge spanning Birk Beck to climb the facing valley side up to Salterwath. Head right through the farmyard and then left to emerge into a field behind the house. The map below provides a detailed resumé of the route back to Scout Green.

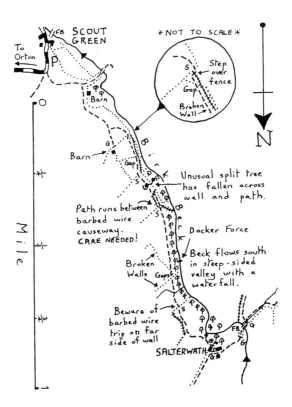

Take a north-west course away from the valley side, descending to a fence, which should be followed to a wall stile. Keep close with the valley rim across a series of walls and fences until the access road from Rampshowe is reached. Bear left up to the metalled road and Scout Green.

All gradients on this walk are easy going and only nonagenarian trekkers should be permitted the excuse of a 'rest' break. For all, the rare phenomenon of total solitude is unequivocally guaranteed.

4. CLAIFE HEIGHTS

Start and Finish: A roadside lay-by on the right of the B5285 a quarter-mile west of Far Sawrey.

Summits Climbed: Latterbarrow   — 803 feet
High Blind How — 882 feet

Total Height Climbed: 1190 feet

Distance Walked: 9 miles

Nearest Centre: Far Sawrey

Map Required: Ordnance Survey English Lakes 1:25000, South East area sheet

INTRODUCTION

The sylvan upland which lies between Lake Windermere and Esthwaite Water provides a rewarding low-level ramble. Those who seek the exhilarating challenge of a remote trek into the unknown will be sadly disappointed by Claife Heights where waymarkers are more profuse than weeds in my back garden. Forestry plantations and natural woodland also ensure that distant views are somewhat restricted. Only the 'monumental' summit of Latterbarrow affords a splendid opportunity for peak spotting across the northern panorama.

One approach to the charming village of Far Sawrey makes use of the Windermere ferry. At one time many locals refused to use the ferry after dark due to a fear of the infamous 'Crier of Claife' whose spirit was eventually exorcised by a Furness monk — or so it was thought. Its influence, however, is still reputed to pervade the vicinity and the ghost is blamed for certain disappearances that have never been satisfactorily explained. He who invades

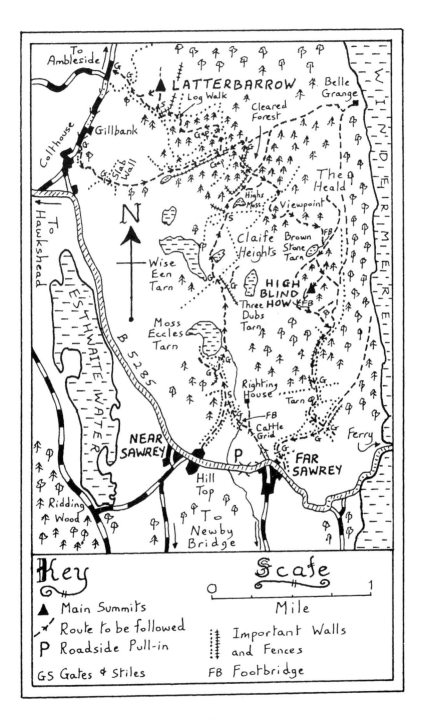

To Ambleside

Colthouse

Gillbank

Slab Wall

To Hawkshead

LATTERBARROW

Log Walk

Cleared Forest

Belle Grange

The Heald

Highs Moss

Viewpoint

Claife Heights

Brown Stone Tarn

FB

Wise Een Tarn

HIGH BLIND HOW

Three Dubs Tarn

FB

Moss Eccles Tarn

WINDERMERE

N

B 5285

ESTHWAITE WATER

Righting House

Tarn

Ferry

NEAR SAWREY

P

FB
Cattle Grid

FAR SAWREY

Hill Top

Ridding Wood

To Newby Bridge

Key

▲ Main Summits

✸ Route to be followed

P Roadside Pull-in

GS Gates & Stiles

Scale

0 — 1
Mile

┇ Important Walls
┇ and Fences

FB Footbridge

the territory of the 'Crier' after dark does so, therefore, at his own peril. You have been warned!

During daylight, this figure of eight walk makes a fine introduction to the more subdued landscape of Silurian Slate country that is characteristic of South Lakeland. Variations in the resistance of the slates to erosion have encouraged the upthrust of rock tors intermingled with low-lying basins containing a myriad of small tarns and reedy pools. This serves as a marked contrast to the naked fell tops normally associated with Lakeland walking.

ROUTE DESCRIPTION

From the lay-by, return along the B5285 to Far Sawrey and turn right up a narrow lane signposted to Colthouse and Wray. Fork left onto a rough track just beyond a cattle grid, the metalled road continuing ahead to Righting House. Over a footbridge the path snakes gradually uphill to be joined by a substantial bridleway coming up from Near Sawrey.

Continue north passing along the east shore of Moss Eccles Tarn, which is more than adequately festooned with signs to warn off unauthorised fisher-folk. Beyond Moss Eccles Tarn, the path heads across open country to approach a straight fence of recent construction. Bear left along the fence to pass through a walled gate. Wise Een Tarn then comes into view across a grassy depression occupied by a brief scattering of trees. Beyond a diminutive reservoir on your right, swing north east up a slope to enter Hollin Band plantation, where the track becomes a forest road.

Leave this where the bridleway forks left alongside a seven-feet high meshed fence of which this area has an inordinate supply. Upon reaching another forest road, head left in a wide sweep around Long Height as far as a rutted track, which bears left into the confines of the forest and is waymarked by guide posts with white toppers.

Over the centuries, much of the natural woodland within the Lake District has disappeared. Nevertheless, ten per cent of the total area is still cloaked in solid tree growth, much of it in the form of coniferous plantings by the Forestry Commission. The period between the Great Wars witnessed the wholesale erection of large unimaginative blocks in the outer valleys including Ennerdale, Grizedale and around Whinlatter Pass. Even though afforestation slows down the process of soil erosion, public opposition to the marching phalanxes has forced the Commission to rethink its policy and come to an agreement that restricts any more heavy duty planting in the core region. The map below gives some idea of how this has worked in practice.

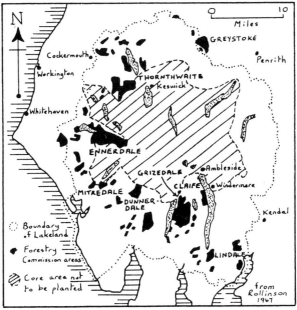

Forestry Commission plantations within the Lake District

Interplanting of different species to break up the drab uniformity has become a welcome feature of present-day forest regeneration. The looser array of trees on much of Claife has had a positive effect on the encouragement of wild life breeding and nature trails. There do, however, exist pockets where all life below the canopy is stifled by close-packed ranks, a dead zone where neither light nor sound can penetrate.

27

After due consideration of the forest scene, continue ahead. Where the open track maintains a forward course as a walled lane after 200 yards, make a right and follow the thin yet obvious trail through dense undergrowth. Zig-zagging up a brief but steep incline and through a wall gap, the path meanders through the forest, eventually crossing a logged section close to the edge of the planting boundary. Bear left along the outer fence until a stile is reached. Over this, head due north up to Latterbarrow whose open prospect is a welcome relief from the cloistered gloom of the forest, a joy to behold. Rest awhile on the numerous rocky ledges before making a descent down the sharp western flank. This merges with a track heading right, which joins the Colthouse road.

Take a left down the road for a half-mile, passing Gillbank, until a gated track on the left points an unerring finger back to Far Sawrey and the ferry. This clear route should be followed until the end of the enclosed lane after which it becomes necessary to retrace your steps along the forest road back around Long Height. Our way continues ahead leaving the abrupt right swing of the road. Entering the darkened recess of a tunnel lined with conifer trunks the trail picks a careful route uphill towards the first viewpoint. Underfoot, the exposed roots clutch like gnarled fingers at one's feet.

The vista above The Heald faces east and provides one of the few points featuring an open aspect. Carry on along the trail to join a forest road close to Brown Stone Tarn. Make a right and soon after a left away from the road. Watch out for an abrupt right turn uphill, which brings us out onto the top of the Heights at High Blind How, where a rocky outcrop supports the stone trig column. Heading south west from this elevated plinth, a footbridge is crossed followed immediately by a short pull up to another rock tor. Head sharp left for an easy descent to the wall that lies atop the eastern slopes, which plunge deep into Lake Windermere.

Make a right at the junction of paths to head south following an initially loose track, which eases on the final stroll back to Far Sawrey. Watch for an abrupt right wheel through a gate at a T-junction of paths before dropping down to merge with the B5285 by a telephone kiosk. Bear right past the hotel for the walk through the village back to the lay-by. Although this is a complicated circuit, it is clear underfoot if rather too overburdened with signposts which discourage visitors from practising the age-old skills associated with map and compass.

5. FORTRESS IN THE SKY

Start and Finish: Two miles south east of Ingleton along the old road, there is a pull-in adjacent to the High Leys access track at GR 719715.

Summit Climbed:	Ingleborough — 2373 feet
Total Height Climbed:	1550 feet
Distance Walked:	6½ miles
Nearest Centre:	Ingleton
Map Required:	Ordnance Survey Yorkshire Dales 1:25000, Western area sheet

INTRODUCTION

Not the most exciting, nor even the most challenging route up Ingleborough, this walk qualifies in being the least known. And undoubtedly, it is also the easiest ascent from valley level of any mountain over 2000 feet in the country, the summit being attained without any slackening of pace. Up to Little Ingleborough, the shepherd's track crosses a bleak moorland wilderness where all is grass pockmarked with craters known as shake holes. These sinks, the result of dissolving limestone, frequently develop into full-blown potholes allowing entry to the extensive subterranean cave system.

The flat plateau, its uniquely stepped contours clearly visible for miles around, was adopted as a defensive site in the early Iron Age by the Brigantes tribe. It survived intact for centuries, bearing witness to their final stand against the Roman invaders in AD 74. Little can now be seen of the crumbling ramparts that trace the rim. Ancient foundations of hut circles are, however, clearly visible at the western edge of the fortress.

29

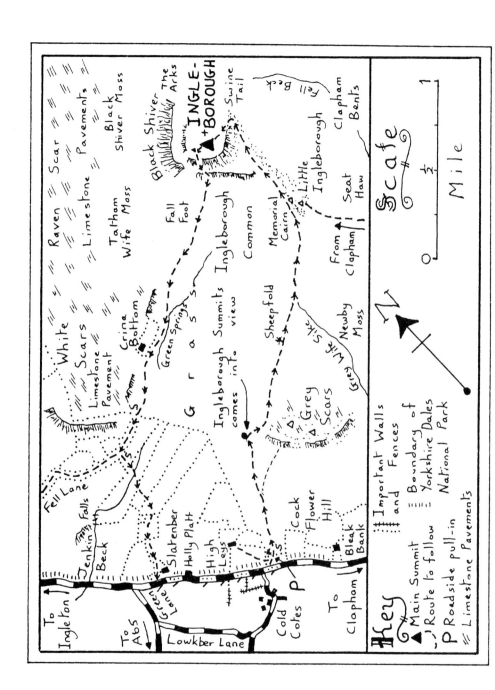

Scale

Mile

Key
- ▲ Main Summit
- ··· Route to follow
- P Roadside pull-in
- ≡ Limestone Pavements
- ⧚ Important Walls and Fences
- ≡ Boundary of Yorkshire Dales National Park

ROUTE DESCRIPTION

From the roadside pull-in, a rough track slants right. Follow it round to a ladder stile in the wall close to some sheep pens. Join a track heading up the grass-clad slopes of Cock Flower Hill (a rather odd name for this lower flank of Ingleborough) parallel to the in-take wall. A right fork along a thin path can be pursued if one wishes to cross the outcropping limestone of Grey Scars, returning to the main track north of a prominent cairn.

Our way slants left of the scars. At a point where the path veers to the east and the in-take wall slopes down towards Crina Bottom, the jutting profile of Ingleborough itself comes into focus.

Passing north of Grey Scars, the grass path heads north east towards the blunted shoulder of Little Ingleborough, passing a stone sheepfold en route. A prominent cairn on the horizon lies below the ridge top adjacent to a slanting rake that blends into the peaty crest. The main track from Clapham should be joined as we head north. After the first limestone collar, the route levels out again before the final climb up the stony eastern rampart of Millstone Grit. After bearing left onto the wide plateau, a series of cairns points the way across the flat expanse to the summit.

Identification of all visible landmarks can be noted using the circular brass mountain plaque topping the cross shelter. Erected by the local fell rescue group in 1953, it is likely to go unnoticed by those visitors not eligible for a first team place with the Harlem Globetrotters.

Our exit from this Iron Age fortress lies to the south west where the encircling fortification is broken. A steep descent of the gritstone cap follows, now substantially eroded and loose. It deserves care so watch your footing. Beyond the next escarpment of shale, the track pursues a direct and gradual course across a peaty moorland keeping left of the White Scars limestone pavement. The track then passes the old farmstead of Crina Bottom.

The path maintains a level course to the right of a dry valley on the approach to the in-take wall. Pass over a stile into the rough walled track known as Fell Lane. After a quarter of a mile, look out for a wooden footpath sign on the left. Cross a stile into the abutting field and follow the wall on your right south into the cutting occupied by Jenkin Beck. At this point, make use of the large-scale map below to allow correct passage through the fields to Slatenber on the old Ingleton-Clapham road.

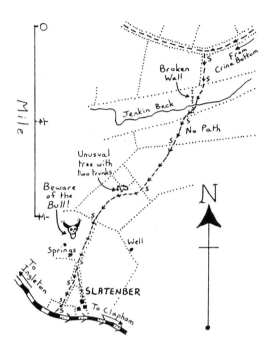

The map is self-explanatory but two points are worthy of further comment. First, the strange pair of trees after the fifth stile appear to have been welded together at their base, giving the appearance of a single tree from afar. Secondly, ample warning is displayed at either side of the bull field as to the resident's aggressive tendencies. On this occasion as I gingerly entered his domain, the indolent fellow had left his concubines to fend for themselves, having eyes only for satisfying the less than erotic needs of his stomach.

At the old road, adjacent to Slatenber, now part of the Yorkshire Dales Cycle Way, turn left towards Clapham for three-quarters of a mile back to the car. This walk provides an easy but positively satisfying afternoon's caper on top of one of the most recognisable peaks in England.

6. AROUND THE LUNE HEADWATERS

Start and Finish: Turn right off the A685 for Ravenstonedale and park at the junction of the first side road on the right at grid reference 717044.

Summits Climbed: Randygill Top — 2047 feet
                              Green Bell   — 1985 feet

Total Height Climbed: 1350 feet

Distance Walked: 8¾ miles

Nearest Centre: Ravenstonedale

Map Required: Ordnance Survey Pathfinder Series
                            1:25000, Tebay and Kirkby Stephen
                            NY 60/70 sheet

INTRODUCTION

Once described as resembling a quiescent herd of elephants, the Howgill Fells present a smoothly undulating appearance, which contrasts markedly with the Lakeland fells. The gently-shelving domes make for easy walking and fast progress can be made along the tractor trails arrowing deep into the fells. Beyond the confines of in-take walls surrounding the valley pastures, there exist no barriers to movement.

Here, only the distant cawing of a lone buzzard, or amiable chatter from silvery-tongued gills, disturb the eternal tranquillity that epitomises all that is best in the Howgills. The school parties and mile-wide paths that have come to dominate more popular destinations have no place in this timeless domain, the rolling panorama having changed but little over the centuries.

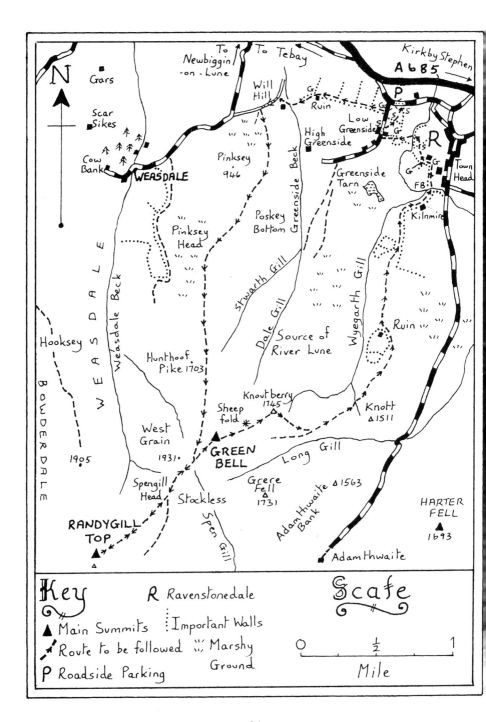

N

Gars

Scar Sikes

Cow Bank

WEASDALE

To Newbiggin-on-Lune

To Tebay

Kirkby Stephen

A685

Will Hill

Ruin

Low Greenside

High Greenside

P

R

Town Head

FB

Kilnmire

Greenside Tarn

Pinksey 946

Pinksey Head

Poskey Bottom

Greenside Beck

Ruin

HOOKSEY

BOWDERDALE

WEASDALE

Weasdale Beck

Strwarth Gill

Dale Gill

Source of River Lune

Wyegarth Gill

1905

Hunthoof Pike 1703

West Grain 1931

Knoutberry 1145

Sheep fold

GREEN BELL

Knott △1511

Long Gill

Spengill Head

Stockless

Grere Fell △ 1731

Adamthwaite △1563 Bank

HARTER FELL

1693

RANDYGILL TOP

Spen Gill

Adamthwaite

Key

R Ravenstonedale

▲ Main Summits

· · · Important Walls

Route to be followed

' '' Marshy Ground

P Roadside Parking

Scale

0   ½   1

Mile

34

ROUTE DESCRIPTION

Make your way up the cul-de-sac serving the Greenside Farms for 100 yards before making a right through a gate. Follow the wall on your left in a westerly direction across the fields until a disintegrating barn is reached. At the old ruin, pass through another gate and change to the other side of the wall. Another gate gives access to a track, which drops down to pass right of the grounds of an old house. Here we cross Greenside Beck to gain a metalled farm road. Now take a left until the accompanying wall veers away right. Where the road enters open terrain, bear left along a tractor track, keeping left around the water-logged depression of Tailor Mire.

Frequent sightings of fell ponies indicate that few other humans are likely to be encountered. These noble beasts deplore the disturbance of their grazing and are likely to regard your presence with disdain.

Indistinct initially, the track heads south south west across the grass flank of Pinksey, becoming more pronounced as height is gradually gained. Continue due south past the lone Hunthoof Pike, crossing the western flank of Green Bell. At the sharp kink in the path, a glance behind will reveal the white trig column of the Bell, one of only three such points that decorate the Howgill tops.

Around the Head of Weasdale, our way lies south west across the broad ridge of Stockless, with our main objective clearly in sight a mile distant. Leave the main track to continue ahead up the narrowing approach to Randygill Top and the breaking of the magical 2000-feet barrier. The substantial cairn often plays host to numerous sheep, who will be rather miffed at having to vacate their favourite perch. Such is the nature of these fells that the permanent occupants have little contact with passing hikers whom they regard as intruders. Note also the small clutch of stones close to the summit exhibiting the well-carved signature of one A. Dodding: 1940 — a wartime soldier on leave, or the local shepherd?

Retrace your steps to mount the distinctive top of Green Bell before carrying on in a north easterly direction down the opposite sloping ridge. Pass a sheepfold on your left and the headwaters of the infant River Lune, which eventually makes an exit beyond Lancaster at Sunderland Point 70 miles distant. A brief rise follows thereafter bringing us onto the gentle outlier of

35

Knoutberry. From here take a course to the south east down its pathless grass slopes, aiming for an obvious path on the far side of Long Gill Valley. Accompany this down under the shadow of Knott, circling to the right of an isolated walled field.

Continue due north to reach the first of the in-take walls after which the track strengthens as it approaches the outer 'suburbs' of Ravenstonedale (Pronounced locally as Rassund'l with a silent 'v') on the right bank of Wyegarth Gill. Join the second span of a double footbridge ascending a grassy lane that opens out into an overgrown excuse for a village green. Stick with the wall on your left before making a right through a gate into a farmyard. At the far end, another gate gives access to a field across which the right of way continues — somewhat indistinct and clearly little used. The large-scale map should be used from here on.

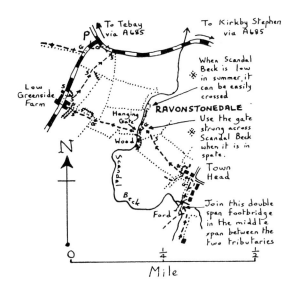

Pass through a wall stile at the far end and drop down to negotiate the waters of Scandal Beck. An old gate appears to be the only access point to cross the beck. In summer when the waters are low, it is no problem to reach the far bank by means of the flat bedrock slabs in the sylvan overhang. In winter, however, the situation requires a cool head and steady nerves.

With the surging waters an ever-present threat, the only possible way forward is to the left along the abutting wall. Head for the edge of a small wood where a sturdy pole and hanging metal gate provide an unorthodox but utterly exciting 'Indiana Jones' type method of gaining the far shore dry-shod.

Climb the opposite bank and follow the accompanying wall on the left. A couple of gates in a direct line bring us to the cluster of farm buildings at Low Greenside. Take a right down the road for no more than 100 yards keeping an eye open for a wall stile on the right giving access to a miniature plantation set in a fenced triangle. Exit by another stile making across the field to the north east and another wall stile. One more field and yet another stile at its far side returns us to the Ravenstonedale access road.

A short right takes you back to your starting point and the culmination of a fine day's hiking.

7. MIST OVER KENTMERE

Start and Finish: A roadside pull-in on the right of High Lane 50 yards before the Bridleway to Longsleddale at grid reference 465050.

Summits Climbed:	Shipman Knotts	— 1908 feet
	Kentmere Pike	— 2397 feet
Total Height Climbed:	1650 feet	
Distance Walked:	5 miles	
Nearest Centre:	Staveley	
Map Required:	Ordnance Survey English Lakes 1:25000, South East area sheet	

INTRODUCTION

Visitors new to the area who learn about the Lake District through glossy brochures may well be forgiven for assuming that blue skies and crystal clear views are standard features. Those of us who know better recognise that days when the fells are obscured by a dense pall of cloud are too numerous to mention. Such conditions tend to discourage the majority of people from venturing aloft.

Yet this ought not to be the case. A hike that is safe, easy to follow underfoot, and not too protracted is most assuredly the answer to those long mist-shrouded days. And with the added attraction of having the fells to yourself, there is much to be enjoyed on a brief foray of the type herein described.

On the day in question, I left home with the aim of completing a low-level ramble as the drizzly blanket had prevented a more ambitious undertaking.

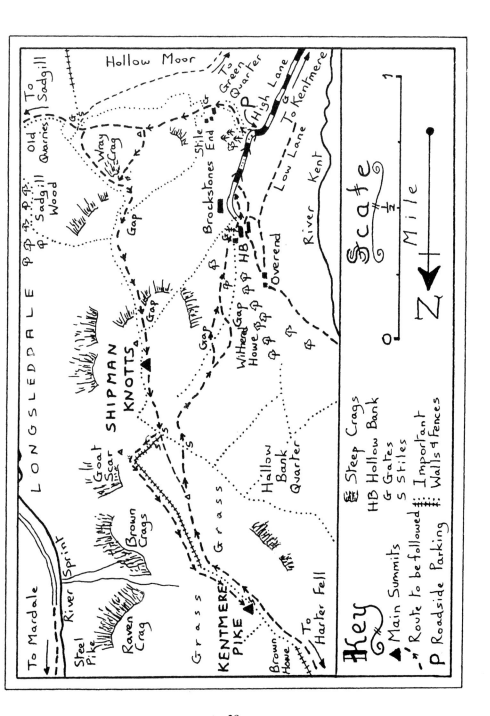

To Mardale

LONGSLEDDALE

Hollow Moor

To Sadgill

Old Quarries

To Green Quarter

High Lane

To Kentmere

River Sprint

Steel Pike

Raven Crag

Brown Crags

Goat Scar

SHIPMAN KNOTTS

Gap

Gap

Gap

Wray Crag

Sadgill Wood

Stile End

Brockstones

HB

Withered Howe

Overend

Low Lane

River Kent

Gap

Grass

Grass

Grass

KENTMERE PIKE

Brown Howe

To Harter Fell

Hollow Bank Quarter

Key

* Main Summits

Route to be followed

P Roadside Parking

Steep Crags

HB Hollow Bank

G Gates

S Stiles

Important Walls & Fences

Scale

0 — ½ — 1 Mile

N

39

Even so, however, visibility was severely restricted. To turn back would have been the simplest alternative but how often was that likely to occur during the long winter months ahead? The decision was quickly made: in for a penny, in for a pound. A hike of some significance might just as well be achieved under the circumstances, so I pressed on to Staveley and up the Kentmere Valley.

Few other vehicles were met en route and no other hikers of like mind were encountered from start to finish. In future, the black rain clouds decorating TV weather maps will elicit no groans of anguish from me so long as hikes of this quality and content can be relished.

ROUTE DESCRIPTION

From the pull-in, make a right up the walled track signposted to Longsleddale abutting a small copse. After passing through a gate, continue ahead past the large barn of Stile End, which is chaperoned by a pair of smaller buildings. Beyond a further gate, the track enters open terrain. Watch for a small cairn on your left that marks an indistinct fork off from the main route.

This recently tramped path initially climbs quite steeply through the lower bracken before graduating on its approach to the rocky enclave of Wray Crag. An abrupt precipitous outcropping, it marks the southern extremity of the Borrowdale Volcanic series. To the south, in sharp contrast, an altogether more subdued landscape of Silurian Slates and gritstones takes over. Gently-shelving heather moorlands that characterise this terrain are more akin to Southern Scotland than classic Lakeland strata.

Where these two types of rock meet, a line of weakness has enabled local farmers to make use of the easy route between Kentmere and Longsleddale. Those who do not wish to venture along the narrow trod should continue ahead to the summit of the pass at 1120 feet. From here, bear left to follow an established trail up Wray Crag, where hands-on contact is necessary to maintain one's equilibrium, especially in wet and greasy conditions.

The wall and fence follows the northbound ridge without interruption and eventually leads to Harter Fell. It provides an invaluable guide when visibility is severely curtailed. Stick with it after surmounting the crag to cross a marshy tract and then up a narrowing stony passage towards Shipman Knotts. The summit proper of this gnarled elbow lies immediately adjacent to the left side of the wall 50 yards beyond a cross wall gap. On my most recent visit, it lacked a suitable cairn until yours truly determined to construct a fitting if rather diminutive monument. Passing hikers are asked to make their own contribution to the burgeoning cairn in order to maintain its stature.

Follow a clear route north until a wall stile is reached after a half-mile. This should be crossed, followed immediately by another over a fence heading north east towards Goat Scar. Accompany this on its right bearing sharp left after 250 yards to pursue a direct course up the broad featureless grass ridge onto Kentmere Pike. For the final quarter of a mile, the fence is abandoned in favour of a substantially constructed wall.

Abutting the trig column, a pair of wooden through steps have been inserted into the wall. Cross to the far side and back-track south east for a half-mile, keeping a watchful eye open for a small cairn. This marks an important highway junction, the right fork of which should be followed down to a wall stile.

The grass track beyond descends an increasingly steep slope passing through an upper wall gap before forking down to merge with the original, if less distinct path, which comes in from the right after passing through its own gap. Maintain a southerly course to arrive at the hamlet of Hallow Bank, which comprises a cluster of traditional farm dwellings. A gate gives access to the valley road, which can then be taken back to the car a quarter-mile distant.

Those who wish to dry themselves off before the roaring fires of a friendly hostelry will have to return to Staveley as the village of Kentmere lost its pub many years ago. The Low Bridge Inn (now a private dwelling) was infamous as the first in England to lose its licence due to the proliferation of drunkenness and immorality. Some things never change, do they?

41

8. PUTTING THE B INTO BLACK COMBE

Start and Finish: A roadside pull-in off the A595 at the farming hamlet of Whitbeck.

Summit Climbed:	Black Combe — 1970 feet
Total Height Climbed:	1950 feet
Distance Walked:	8½ miles
Nearest Centre:	Bootle
Map Required:	Ordnance Survey Pathfinder Series 1:25000, SD 08/18 sheet

---

INTRODUCTION

Although located at the southernmost tip of the National Park, Black Combe assumes the same geological characteristics as its jovial cousin to the north. This outcropping of Skiddaw Slate presents a gently rippled appearance, with its brittle flaky texture being the oldest rock type in the Lake District.

Every season has its finer qualities but, for me, late summer is difficult to surpass as the abundant greens of earlier months begin to fade. From Broughton-in-Furness, the south-facing slopes take on a patchwork tapestry encompassing all manner of natural tints as autumn approaches.

From on high, the fell has received numerous credits for the breadth of its panorama. Colonel Mudge, a 19th-century surveyor in the Royal Artillery, claimed for it a more extensive view than any other point in Britain. And no less a person than William Wordsworth also dedicated a graphic ode to it in

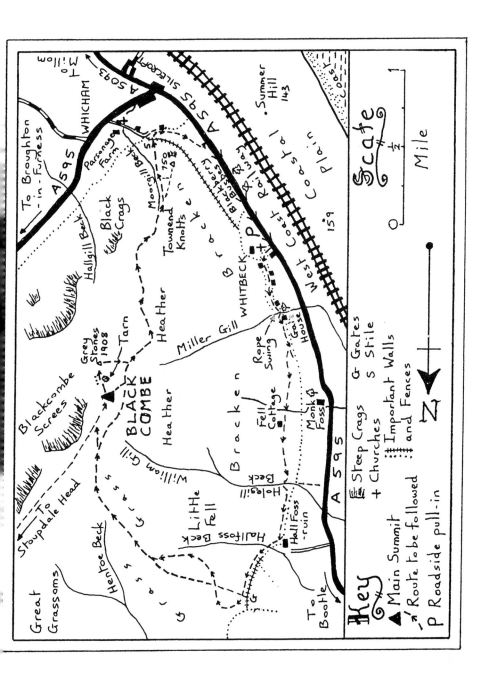

Scale

0   ½   1

Mile

Key

▲ Main Summit

↗ Route to be followed

P Roadside pull-in

🗻 Steep Crags

+ Churches

G Gates

S Stile

‡‡‡ Important Walls
and Fences

N

1813 entitled, 'View from the Top of Black Combe', two verses of which are included here:

> Close by the sea, lone sentinel,
> Black Combe his forward station keeps;
> He breaks the sea's tumultuous swell, —
> And ponders o'er the level deeps.
>
> He listens to the bugle horn,
> Where Eskdale's lovely valley bends;
> Eyes Walney's early fields of corn;
> Sea-birds to Holker's woods he sends.

No mountain in England lies closer to the sea, or to the Isle of Man.

ROUTE DESCRIPTION

Make your way north along the lay-by, taking a right turn beside Whitbeck Church, which is faced with local red sandstone. This old road soon bears left to run parallel with the new highway built to accommodate the increase in road traffic. Connecting a diversity of old cottages, it gives an intimate glimpse into the orientation of the antiquated north-bound route. The sharp western slope of the fell is clearly evident here where it falls away to the narrow coastal plain. This flat coastal area results from a violent clash between the New Red Sandstone and the Skiddaw Slate.

Where the track bends acutely to cross Miller Gill adjacent to Gate House, a dangling rope swing enables you to add a little excitement to your life. Having thus crossed the gill, continue along the track, which climbs through bracken whilst veering away from the in-take wall.

Beyond Fell Cottage, the path rejoins the wall to cross Holegill Beck, after which the ruined farmhouse of Hall Foss is passed. At this point opposite Barfield Tarn, the route suddenly begins to climb. The wall soon gives way to a fence. Follow this until it merges with another coming up from valley level. Fork right off the main path to circle back, heading south up the grassy swathe of Little Fell. The way then bears left into the higher cutting, which marks the source of Hallfoss Beck. As the track fades in the bilberry and grass, maintain an easterly bearing to merge with another path that climbs gradually across the bleak moorland.

This is not the sort of terrain to be caught napping in when the mist descends. If such, however, is your choosing or misfortune, then a south-easterly course will eventually bring you to the abrupt rim of Blackcombe Screes. A mile of broken cliffs supports the dark scooped hollows, which give this great sprawling fell its name, and are in stark contrast to the extensive smoothed appearance of the northern slopes.

Even when smoke can be seen rising straight up from farmhouse chimneys in the valley, a keen unbroken wind always seems to blow across the exposed summit from the Irish Sea. The large shelter abutting a trig column provides welcome relief and makes an ideal spot for lunch.

Beyond the summit, cross a depression housing a small reedy tarn, and then on to the subsidiary summit of Grey Stones. This sports a man-made dais of substantial proportions. Unfortunately, it is now beginning to disintegrate on one side due to the mountaineering activities of some careless souls. From here, head west to join the main track bound for Whicham. The way is clear along a flaky track. The blooming heather brings a splash of delicate purple to the dusky mountain flanks.

Ahead, the proximity of the sea gives you the illusion of being able to dive straight in from Townend Knotts. The path descends the left side of this promontory and down the dell of Moorgill Beck. Beyond a fence stile, continue ahead, passing right of a dwelling prior to swinging north west through the bracken below an accompanying fence. Follow a thin trod, which brings you out onto the main road north of Silecroft.

9. WHERNSIDE — THE NORTH FACE

Start and Finish: The grass verge beside Deepdale Methodist Chapel, which can be found 1 ¼ miles south east of Dent village at GR 722859.

Summit Climbed:	Whernside	— 2419 feet
Total Height Climbed:	1800 feet	
Distance Walked:	8 miles	
Nearest Centre:	Dent	
Map Required:	Ordnance Survey Yorkshire Dales 1:25000, Western area sheet	

INTRODUCTION

The side valley of Kingsdale, which marks the western limit of Whernside, is somewhat neglected by the majority of travellers heading into the Dales by way of Ingleton. A lonely dale isolated from the ravages of time, it frustrates easy passage by means of a number of road gates, which must be opened and assiduously closed to maintain farm boundaries throughout its length. Arrow-straight for almost three miles, the narrow highway traces a discreet line between grey layers of scarred limestone rising abruptly on either flank. The grass path is indistinct and only lightly worn, unlike that on the east side of the mountain where boot erosion has reached epidemic proportions.

Whernside's summit lies hidden from view until the main section of the ridge is gained. There is little likelihood of your being the sole occupant there. In fine weather, all manner of sun seekers will be encountered, reclining along the edge overlooking Ribblehead — a splendid vantage point if you are fortunate enough to be present when the celebrated Settle-Carlisle train

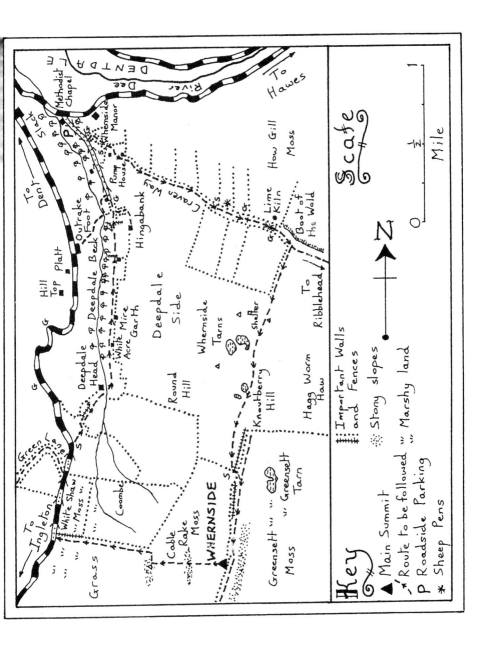

trundles over Batty Moss viaduct. Thankfully the future of this most illustrious of highland railways seems assured, a welcome asset for Dales folk and all who visit the area.

ROUTE DESCRIPTION

Tucked away from casual view, Deepdale Methodist Chapel lies hidden in its own secluded glade and is easily missed. Park on the grass verge and head south east up Dyke Hall Lane for a quarter of a mile as far as a rough track on the left. A gate is soon reached, after which turn immediate right to climb the walled corridor. Beyond a ladder stile, the track bears right away from the accompanying wall, initially on concrete. A small water pumping house is passed on the left at the rear of which is a peep hole to observe metered flow. Above, two fenced springs provide evidence of traditional sources of water before the era of plastic pipe and electric pump.

The path soon meets a wall, which accompanies it on the left for a half-mile before its fully walled status is resumed. Negotiation of a ladder stile is followed by two gates further on. Immediately prior to the second gate, another on the left allows access to explore a noteworthy lime kiln. Having passed through the sheep pens contained within the corridor, the path enters open country with the wall on the right for the first 200 yards. This track, known as the Craven Way, continues above a low scar to Ribblehead. Having once been an essential link with Dent, it now provides a quick and easy route for walkers.

Turn right at the wall corner to pursue a thin trail, which maintains a south-south-westerly course towards Whernside Tarns, passing close to a significant cairn and shelter 200 yards on the right. When the track fades, bear left around the eastern edge of the tarns to pick up a strengthening path. This makes a gradual ascent towards the left corner where a wall and fence converge ahead. Cross the stile and a gap in the parallel broken wall to join a well-worn path heading south along the steep rim of Knoutberry Hill.

Below the abrupt downfall, Greensett Tarn shimmers in the afternoon sunlight, a jewel in the crown largely ignored by the majority of visitors. Continue up the ridge alongside the wall, which makes a distinct kink at

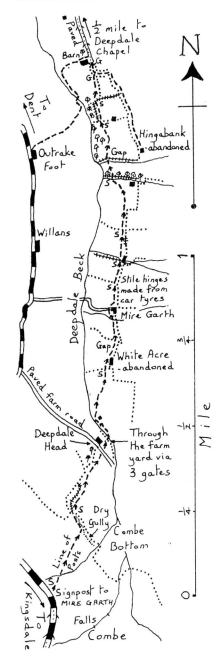

the summit. A narrow gap allows access to the west side and the triangulation column.

Head due west from the summit along a clear grass path, which descends gently for a quarter-mile before reaching the first of two rough steps. Here the steepening path is loose and care is needed. Levelling out below, the way continues on grass to a prominent cairn on the edge of the second step. Make a right here along the lip to a wall corner and turn left to accompany an unswerving line down to the Kingsdale road on a faint path.

Head right for half a mile along the road until it bears left on the descent into Deepdale. Watch out for a stile on the right signposted to Mire Garth. From this point, make use of the large-scale map opposite on this final section of the walk. Cross the stile to descend the grass slopes of White Shaw on a thin path, the course of which is marked by a series of wooden posts. Upon reaching a groove with a further signpost, bear left down the rim to cross a wall stile. Follow the fence down the lower pastures to the working farm of Deepdale Head.

Across the concrete road, a bright yellow footpath sign acts as a homing beacon. Turn right through the gate across the farmyard and immediately through a double gate to continue north through the fields. Bear left of an isolated stone building beyond the farm, then half right over the fields towards the abandoned farm of White Acre. Another yellow sign indicates a deviation from the expected route through a wall stile left of the derelict buildings.

Keep left of the north-bound wall through a gap passing to the left of Mire Garth. Stick with the wall over three further stiles until a large stone barn is reached adjoining a wooded tributary. Bear left towards the main valley beck, crossing the narrow watercourse followed immediately by a ladder stile. The fence alongside the next tributary has been trampled down so walk straight across, after which a slight rise around a copse is required.

Beyond two further stiles, a gate gives access to Dyke Hall Lane, here walled and unpaved. Bear left for 100 yards through another gate, passing a new barn on the left, after which the lane becomes metalled. Follow it for three-quarters of a mile back to Deepdale Chapel.

10. ALONE AROUND LOWESWATER

Start and Finish: Approaching the hamlet of Loweswater from Lorton Vale, a fork in the road adjacent to a telephone box provides parking for four cars.

Summits Climbed:	Low Fell	— 1375 feet
	Darling Fell	— 1270 feet

Total Height Climbed: 1400 feet

Distance Walked: 6 miles

Nearest Centre: High Lorton

Map Required: Ordnance Survey English Lakes 1:25000, North West area sheet

INTRODUCTION

Tucked away in the north-west corner of the Lake District, Low Fell and its surrounding fells all lie under 1400 feet in stature. Visitors approaching from the north down Lorton Vale have little time or inclination to give these smoothly curving hills more than just a passing glance, their eyes focussed with anticipation on the dramatic scene unfolding beyond Crummock.

These fells surrounding the secluded expanse of Loweswater tend, therefore, to be overshadowed by their more illustrious colleagues to the south. Loweswater and its environs have little in common with the bustling activity that characterises most of the other lakes. It remains a timeless enclave, quiet and unassuming, and uncommercialised.

Here then exists a landscape designed for the solitary walker, who can rest content in the knowledge that the fells will be his alone for the day.

51

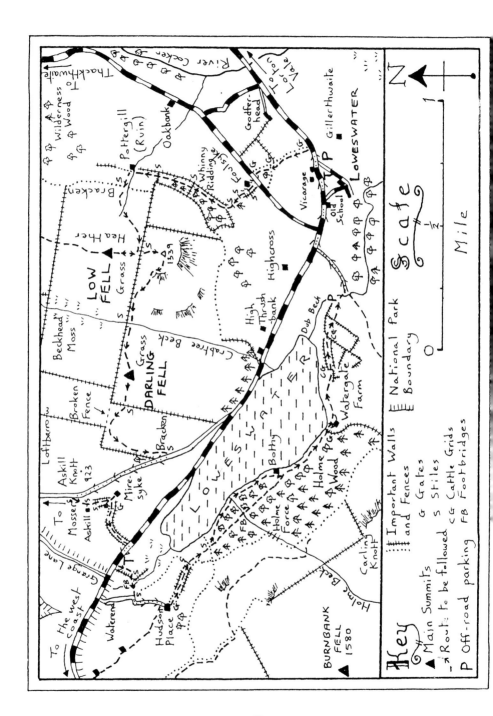

Key
:::: Important Walls and Fences
≡ National Park Boundary
▲ Main Summits
G Gates   S Stiles
⇢ Route to be followed   CG Cattle Grids
P Off-road parking   FB Footbridges

Scale
0   ½   1
Mile

52

Unfortunately, the fell wanderer's normal expectation of free passage across the upland tract is hampered by the enthusiastic use of fencing. This geometric parcelling-out is a feature dating back to medieval times when the farmers of Mosser were first permitted grazing rights by their patron, Richard de Lucy. Even though the forest has long since disappeared, the established boundaries of pasturage are still relevant and should be respected.

ROUTE DESCRIPTION

From the telephone box, return along the road for 50 yards until a signpost on the left points the way through a gate across the fields. Follow the wall on your right through another gate and thence up to the Thackthwaite road. Turn left here and almost immediately right along Mosser Fell Road. This rough track passes Foulsyke, being hedged on both sides. Many of the indicated fences on the map are also hedged in the valley pastures, the dry-stone wall being a rare phenomenon in this sector of the National Park.

After a quarter of a mile and three stiles, the route swings right along the wooded base of Low Fell, which rises sharply on your left. Leave the edge of the wood after a further half-mile by crossing over a stile, and approach the abandoned farmstead of Pottergill, now only a ruin. At this point it is necessary to tackle the soaring east flank alongside a chattering beck. Although it is under 1400 feet, Low Fell rises steeply and it should be tackled at a steady if sedate pace.

A path soon emerges on the left of the stream and winds uphill through the bracken to a rare wall, which contours along the slope. Beyond the wall stile the path fades as height is gained. Cross the beck when the bracken carpet thins, bearing left to meet the upcoming fence. The crest of the main north-south ridge is soon reached thereafter.

Head right along a good path and on to the highest point of Low Fell, which is surmounted by a cairn but displays little else of immediate interest. Return south to the fence and cross the stile giving access to the subsidiary though much superior summit. As a viewpoint, it is exceptional. Here is revealed for the first time the mellow quiescence that is Loweswater.

In the foreground of the splendid panorama, Mellbreak strives hard to catch the eye. One's gaze, however, is inevitably drawn to the surging might of Grasmoor across the vale. Beyond Crummock Water, the tantalising waters of Buttermere peep out from behind Rannerdale Knotts. Without doubt, Low Fell provides a marvellous viewpoint from which to absorb at leisure the contrasting extremes of this lovely valley.

To reach Darling Fell, head west dodging between low outcrops and keeping right to regain the fence, which pursues an arrow-straight course across the rolling terrain. Cross the deep rift hewn by the erosive power of Crabtree Beck, continuing up the opposite slope. A slight deviation is needed to bring you onto this neighbouring summit. All is grass hereabouts with indigenous rocks being few and far between. Those used in the construction of the substantial cairn have been shipped in from the rough western flank.

Continue along the western ridge, across a fence stile and down the slope, returning to the main fence line as it heads towards Askill Knott. Swing left along a thin path cutting through the bracken and down the steep banking to emerge into Mosser Lane. Head right up this narrow metalled highway, which has a grass band growing down the middle.

After a third of a mile, cross the stile, which gives access to a rough link track descending gradually to the main Loweswater road via a series of stiles and gates. Take a left along the road for 100 yards past a telephone box, before entering a field on the left. Peer along the hedge, noting a low sign that points the way right across an abutting field. A useful plank causeway on either side of a foot bridge enables a dry-footed crossing of marshland at Waterend.

Join the access lane to Hudson Place, passing the farmhouse to enter a rough fenced lane, which brings us to Holme Wood. After entering the glade, fork left along an easy-going trail that meanders by the lake side. Beyond the stone bothy, rejoin the main track, leaving the wooded copse at Watergate Farm.

The farm track brings us to Maggie's Bridge after which the road is metalled. At the main road, take a right past the old school and vicarage back to the start.

11. THE SPIRIT OF MALLERSTANG

Start and Finish: Wide roadside pull-ins provide ample parking space on the B6259 opposite the side lane known locally as Tommy Road and close to Pendragon Castle.

Summit Climbed: High Seat   — 2328 feet

Total Height Climbed: 1600 feet

Distance Walked: 9 miles

Nearest Centre: Outhgill

Map Required: Ordnance Landranger Series 91 1:50,000, Appleby-in-Westmorland sheet

INTRODUCTION

A secluded and wholly enchanting valley, Mallerstang receives few mentions in tourist guides, remaining a backwater devoted to agrarian pursuits. It is an ideal location, therefore, for the lone fell wanderer. Outhgill is the only settlement of any consequence, and that little more than a hamlet. The name, derived from the Norse meaning 'desolate ravine', testifies to the bleak nature of the extensive fell country above the in-take walls.

The valley must have been witness to much turmoil in the past if the line of decaying castles is anything to go by. Standing gaunt and abandoned, these once-proud sentinels offer a tantalising glimpse of the violent drama that was once played out beneath the weathered gritstone edges.

Pendragon Castle is the most easily visited, lying as it does adjacent to our roadside pull-in. Reputed to have been the birthplace of Uther Pendragon,

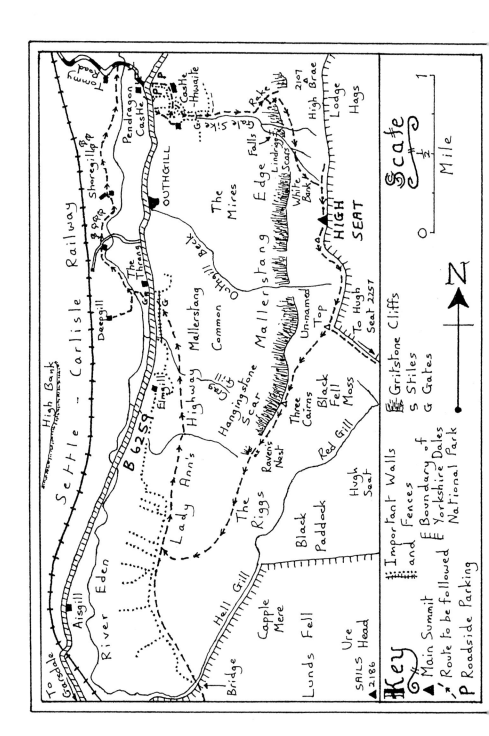

Key

Main Summit

Route to be followed

P Roadside Parking

Important Walls and Fences

Boundary of Yorkshire Dales National Park

Gritstone Cliffs

S Stiles

G Gates

Scale

½ Mile

father of the fabled King Arthur, it was later occupied by Lady Anne Clifford. This remarkable lady was the daughter of an Elizabethan adventurer and owned numerous castles in north-west England, which have all fallen into disrepair apart from that at Skipton. It is no wonder that ghostly images from a tempestuous past make their presence felt at every turn of winding trail.

ROUTE DESCRIPTION

Head south along the B6259 for no more than 100 yards before entering an open field through a gate. Crossing the field obliquely right, the pathless bridleway terminates in a blocked stile, which requires climbing in order to gain access to the rough walled lane beyond. It does not need a budding Sherlock to deduce that few people ever pass this way. However, to avoid damaging the crops, the most sensible alternative is perhaps to make use of the Castlethwaite farm road just to the north.

A right swing up to the adjacent farm will bring you to an impenetrable barrier of nettles, where the right of way passes left behind the garage. Instead, bear left after negotiating the blocked stile to pass through a gate and then right into another lane. This climbs through the trees before emerging into a broad walled passage leading up to the open fell. Beyond a final gate, Gale Sike is crossed and followed upstream towards the overhang of Lindrigg Scars. Pathless and somewhat confusing for the newcomer, this initial phase is well illustrated on the large-scale map overleaf.

As the base of the crag is approached, watch out for a grooved rake slanting left up the fell side. Leave Gale Sike to swing left up the rake until another makes a sharp right to zig-zag onto the upper slopes above the main cliff. Cross the tributaries of the Sike and ascend the blunted prow of White Bank, which brings us onto the bleak plateau above Mallerstang Edge.

Half a mile to the south east lies High Seat, the highest point along the Mallerstang rim, yet barely elevated from the surrounding peat-hagged wilderness. All is trackless until a faint path is located heading south along the crest. After a brief upward stroll, the cairn is reached and a full grandstand view east encompassing the entire panoply of Dales symmetry is revealed.

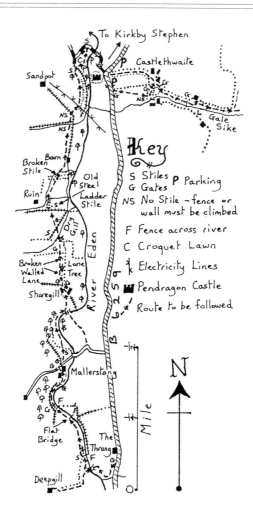

To Kirkby Stephen

Castlethwaite

Sandpot

Gale
Sike

Key

Broken
Stile

Old
Steel
Ladder
Stile

Ruin

S Stiles   P Parking
G Gates
NS No Stile – fence or
      wall must be climbed
F Fence across river
C Croquet Lawn
⚡ Electricity Lines
Pendragon Castle
Route to be followed

Broken
Walled
Lane

Barn

Lone
Tree

Shoregill

River Eden

Mallerstang

N

Mile

Flat
Bridge

The
Thrang

Deepgill

Westward across the deep trough of the Upper Eden, Wild Boar presents a far
more arresting profile and commands attention to the exclusion of all else.

From the subsidiary cairn, a long sweep left around the headwaters of
Outhgill Beck brings you to the more substantial summit, which unfortunately remains nameless. Any suggestions? The faintness of the trails is a good
indicator that few souls pass this way; and it should be added that this desolate
expanse of featureless moorland cannot be recommended in mist. Straying

from the indistinct route in such conditions might easily result in your bleached bones lying undiscovered until Uther Pendragon returns to claim his birthright.

The ridge path heads south east along the unmarked National Park boundary to circle Black Fell Moss bound for Hugh Seat. Our way lies south west along a clear path following the abrupt edge of Hangingstone Scar. A trio of cairns stand alone and forlorn on the very lip of the drop. Their purpose forgotten, they no doubt commemorate a local event, which some astute and knowledgeable reader might wish to impart to this ignorant soul.

Continue along until the gritstone downfall blends unobtrusively into the grass sward. Beyond the stony cluster of Raven's Nest, the path fades into the landscape as you descend The Riggs. Below right, the upper in-take wall marks the course of Lady Anne's Highway, the original valley route much used by drovers and even horse-drawn carriages before the advent of the modern turnpike. Well drained and pursuing a gentle gradient, the old road avoids the swampy bottomland from which Mallerstang gets its name (marsh of the wild duck). Join it by swinging west over the Common before heading back north in company with the spirits of a myriad of by-gone travellers.

Take your time on the protracted descent to the valley road, emerging by way of a fence gate. Cross over immediately before The Thrang Country Hotel and pass through a gate, taking the far road signposted to Deepgill. Upon crossing the River Eden, make a right to follow the path northward, a right of way that frequently fades but is easily followed when the accompanying large-scale map is referred to.

Pass the clutch of old farm buildings known as Shoregill. Once in terminal decline, this tiny hamlet has been restored and settled by "offcomers" from outside the area. At the far end of the route, the ancient game of croquet is still practised and visitors are requested to circumvent the lawn, thus protecting the billiard table smoothness of the green. Beyond, join Tommy Road and make a right to return to your starting point.

Having completed the walk, a final visit to Pendragon Castle will help to maintain the illusion of magic so easily conjured up in Mallerstang.

12. THE 'MITE' OF FELL AND FOREST

Start and Finish: Eskdale Green is well endowed with free parking spaces in contrast to many other Lakeland villages.

Summits Climbed:	Whin Rigg	— 1755 feet
	Illgill Head	— 1983 feet
	Boat How	— 1105 feet

Total Height Climbed: 2250 feet

Distance Walked: 11½ miles

Nearest Centre: Eskdale Green

Map Required: Ordnance Survey English Lakes 1:25000, South West area sheet

INTRODUCTION

In startling contrast to the forested slopes of lower Miterdale, the wind-swept green blanket surrounding Burnmoor Tarn provides exhilarating exercise. Although this is a fairly long walk, the gently shelving terrain enables the miles to be eaten up at a rapid pace.

This is a vast rolling wilderness to the east of Whin Fell, with immense rock turrets surging up from the sombre depths of Wastwater. The wide summit ridge provides a wonderful viewpoint for the mightiest peaks in Lakeland. Westwards, the landscape softens to merge with the coastal plain, and the eye is constantly drawn to the man-made edifice of Sellafield.

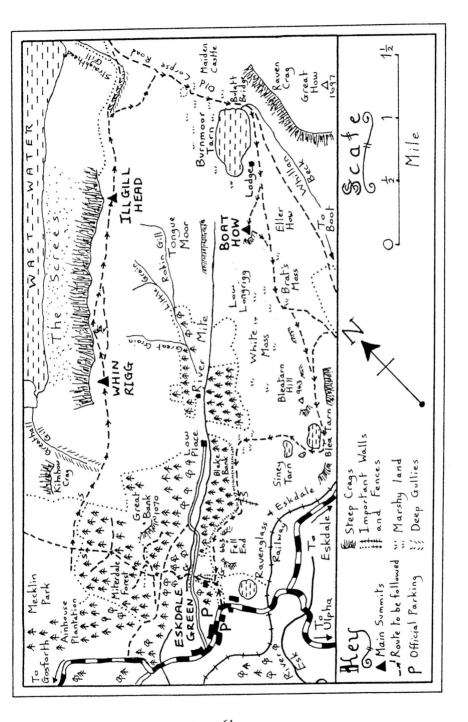

Key

▲ Main Summits
⌁ Route to be followed
P Official Parking

𝔐 Steep Crags
∴ Important Walls and Fences
≀ Marshy land
⋙ Deep Gullies

Scale

0 — ½ — 1 — 1½
Mile

N

Bleak indeed is the terrain encompassing Burnmoor Tarn. An eerie world of grass moorland, it is little wonder that the Old Corpse Road is apt to despatch a cold shiver down the spine at the thought of those cadavers jolting across the lonely tract bound from Wasdale for a consecrated burial. When the mist draws a curtain over the rippling waters and the wind screams its mournful lament, beware the Burnmoor Ghost that haunts this trail, a spectral horse galloping apace with a coffin strapped to its back.

ROUTE DESCRIPTION

From Eskdale Green, take the rough-walled lane alongside the Outward Bound School and follow it round to cross the Miterdale road. Flanked on its lower reaches by deciduous woodland, this forgotten valley remains a secret cherished by the discerning few. The upper slopes are now awash with conifer plantations and a clear track meanders steadily upwards through the dense wood.

Amongst the trees, all is silent. Even footsteps become muted by the thick carpet of pine needles. On all sides vertical boles close in, their wizened arms clutching in an effort to ensnare the unwise intruder who ventures into this twilight world. Breaks in the forest canopy have allowed delicate rock gardens to prosper. In late summer particularly, vivid splashes of gorse yellow complement the purple heather to create a natural tapestry of distinction that no landscape gardener could emulate.

Eventually the bleat of sheep mingled with birdsong assures us that the open fell is close to hand. Cross a stile and continue ahead for 50 yards before heading right to follow a path along the upper forest boundary wall. Beyond another wall stile, maintain an easterly bearing to mount a shallow rise before descending to the head of Greathall Gill ravine on your left.

Climb the left side of the ridge, keeping the summit of Whin Rigg in view all the way. The cairn teeters on the brink of the abrupt cliff top, a stunning prospect along Wastwater now unfolding. Keep to the trail that winds precariously along the rim of cliffs for the first half-mile, before veering away to pursue a direct course along the broad shoulder of cropped turf and so up

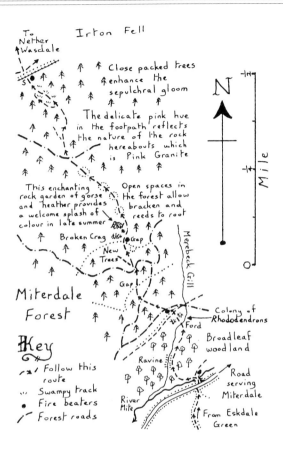

on to Illgill Head. A featureless plateau, it nevertheless provides a wonderful view of Wasdale Head and the surrounding fells.

The path towards Wasdale Head descends the north-east ridge and should be taken until it closes with a wall at the apex of a gully carved out by Straighthead Gill. From here, take the narrow trail heading right. This drops down over heathery slopes to merge with the Old Corpse Road across spongy ground at its highest point. Bear right along this well-used if somewhat macabre highway heading towards the large expanse of Burnmoor Tarn.

Marshy on all sides, the track crosses the shallow beds of inlet streams prior to crossing Bulatt Bridge and then swinging due south bound for

63

Eskdale. Leave the Old Corpse Road, forking right on a clear grass path that rises gradually past the Lodge across the featureless eastern flank of Boat How. Watch for an indistinct path branching right, which makes a beeline for this final summit.

From afar, Boat How presents the appearance of a flat rock cap, an exposed oasis amidst the verdant moor. Its jaunty perch commands the head of Miterdale to the south west and gives the illusion of being stranded on a desert island surrounded by a grass sea.

A direct crossing of White Moss, although contemplated, was discarded in favour of this longer but infinitely drier alternative. Before rejoining the main track, those who are interested in ancient relics might wish to visit the numerous stone circles hereabouts. When the track over Brat's Moss swings left, watch for a thinner path forking right before the main route begins its descent to Boot. Take this short cut along the edge of White Moss, following a level course between irregular outcrops. It soon merges with an old miners' track slanting up from the valley.

Stick with this clear trail past Bleatarn Hill and down to circle behind Blea Tarn. Bear north west, keeping right of Siney Tarn to gain the upper forest boundary wall/fence, where a wide causeway gives access to Miterdale Bottom. Accompany the forest edge south west for its entire length, crossing a fence stile, and thence through high bracken, squeezed by the rocky palisade of Fell End. Pass into a gated lane to rejoin the outward route after 50 yards. Make a left here and return to the car park and toilets at Eskdale Green.

13. GUARDIANS OF SEDBERGH

Start and Finish: Immediately beyond the main one-way cobbled street of Sedbergh heading east on the A683, unrestricted parking is allowed.

Summits Climbed:	Arant Haw	— 1989 feet
	Calders	— 2214 feet
	Great Dummacks	— 2160 feet

Total Height Climbed: 1700 feet

Distance Walked: 8 miles

Nearest Centre: Sedbergh

Map Required: Ordnance Survey Pathfinder Series 1:25000, Sedbergh & Baugh Fell sheet SD 69/79

INTRODUCTION

Fell wandering in Northern England requires copious helpings of the most essential of all ingredients — eternal optimism. Ignore the falling barometer and take to the hills.

Sandwiched between the Lake District and Yorkshire Dales, the Howgills remain staunchly aloof. Their individual silky smooth character offers solitude that is fast becoming a rare phenomenon in their famed counterparts. Like a school of sleeping dolphins enjoying a siesta, they exude an aura of tranquillity that only attracts those who enjoy their own company. Massed ranks of parading walkers have no place here.

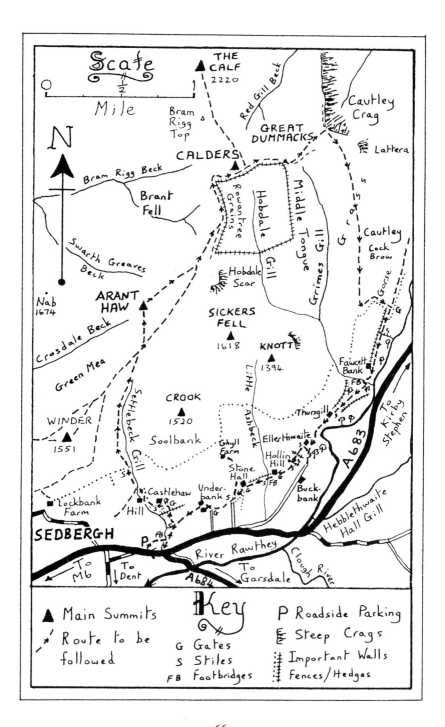

The Howgills lack walls above the in-take fields as well as any particular distinguishing features, and this means that special care must always be taken when walking in heavy mist. The ever-present danger of losing your way in bad conditions must never be underestimated. Even with the help of map and compass, it remains far from easy to maintain a correct course when all is grass amidst a rolling terrain.

ROUTE DESCRIPTION

Take the footpath on the left of the A683 to pass behind a small housing estate. It emerges onto a rough lane after crossing the lower reaches of Settlebeck Gill by a footbridge. Bear left until a wrought-iron kissing-gate on the left gives access to the field path. Follow this up a gentle slope through a fence gate. Swing left through another gate and on to Castlehaw. A well-used track bears right up the fenced and wooded mid-course of the Gill. Cross to the left bank advancing up to the stile in the in-take wall.

Open country lies ahead. The path climbs north above Settlebeck Gill on the east flank of Winder, one of three fells in the district that sports a white concrete trig column. Emerging from the confines of the ravine, the path joins the well-trodden route from Howgill Lane, the old Roman Road. Head north east, taking a left fork after 200 yards, which pursues a direct northerly cut onto Arant Haw. An undistinguished huddle of stones crowns the summit with little else to halt progress.

So continue north east along the broad saddle to rejoin the main track as it drops down to the col of Rowantree Grains alongside a fence. This lone enclosure forms the western side of a giant sheepfold, which occupies the whole of Upper Hobdale. On either side of the col, steep grass slopes fall away acutely, preventing direct access to the tops. This is a feature of these hills and is frequently overlooked by those who think only rock can be precipitous.

The path continues up the facing bank on the left of the fence, prior to swinging sharp right up onto Calders. Protruding from the substantial cairn like a medieval pike, an iron post is first seen marking the highest point slightly adrift from the fence. With your back against the mound of stones and sheltered from a biting westerly, this makes a good lunch stop. Ahead, the way leads down Middle Tongue into Hobdale, or over Great Dummacks. I made for Great Dummocks, not having visited it previously, and so headed off east along the fence.

Swinging south at the Top of Middle Tongue, our way forks left along a thin trail, which is soon abandoned if the highest point of the fell is to be crossed. Capped with a rough thatch of heather and bilberry, Great Dummacks must claim the booby prize as one of the least interesting summits in the country. It has no cairn and merely acts as the shoulder pad for the more eminent Calders. It does, however, possess one redeeming feature, which is revealed in all its glory beyond the horizon — the splintered rock wall of Cautley Crag.

Leaving the upper circle, follow a thin trail down the south ridge. Before you lies the Rawthey with its lovely wooded banks, the in-take wall marking the sudden divergence from wild barren moorland. When the wall is neared, bear left to join it and descend the increasingly steep grass slope of Cock Brow. A slow measured tack is recommended on this section.

Once the main bridleway is gained, head right alongside a fence for Fawcett Bank, once abandoned but now providing refurbished accommodation to a new generation of rustic dwellers. The road beyond crosses Hobdale Beck by a narrow bridge in a delightful wooded glen, and thereafter continues to Thursgill Farm. At this point, the Rawthey forces its way through a constricting ravine that gives excellent sport for white-water chasers.

From here, the old road heads for Ellerthwaite where a slight deviation to the right of way should be noted. Now avoiding a 'cage club of cacophonous canines', it leaves the farm track on your right over a stile, crossing a field to continue alongside hedges to Hollin Hill. After crossing Little Ashbeck by a footbridge, head for Stone Hall. Join a paved access road here until it veers due south to meet the A683. Look for a hidden stile on the right and carry on through the fields to the cluster of renovated farm buildings known as Underbank. Beyond the last cottage, a rough hedged lane takes us directly back to the outer suburbs of Sedbergh, emerging onto the A683 opposite the entrance to Settlebeck High School.

Make a right here to rejoin your car and the culmination of a hike encompassing starkly contrasting scenery. From the bleak wind-swept uplands through verdant valley pastures, this trek has it all.

14. THE ALTERNATIVE BORROWDALE

Start and Finish: A lay-by on the A6 with adjacent telephone kiosk situated a quarter-mile south of where it crosses Borrowdale Beck.

Summits Climbed:		
	Winterscleugh	— 1522 feet
	Whinfell Beacon	— 1544 feet
	Castle Fell	— 1560 feet
	Mabbin Crag	— 1580 feet
	Ashstead Fell	— 1530 feet

Total Height Climbed: 2150 feet

Distance Walked: 10½ miles

Nearest Centre: Kendal

Map Required: Ordnance Survey English Lakes 1:25000, South East area sheet

INTRODUCTION

Unlike its more famous Lakeland cousin, the Whinfell Borrowdale has always retained an aura of mystery, and visitors have tended to be dissuaded walking in this desolate landscape. Commercial enterprise has however been quick to take advantage of Borrowdale's lack of National Park status, with the erection of not one but two communications masts here, which become eyesores visible for miles around.

The north side of the valley still thankfully remains totally unspoilt and must rate highly amongst the few pathless open tracts of wilderness that have so far escaped any form of exploitation.

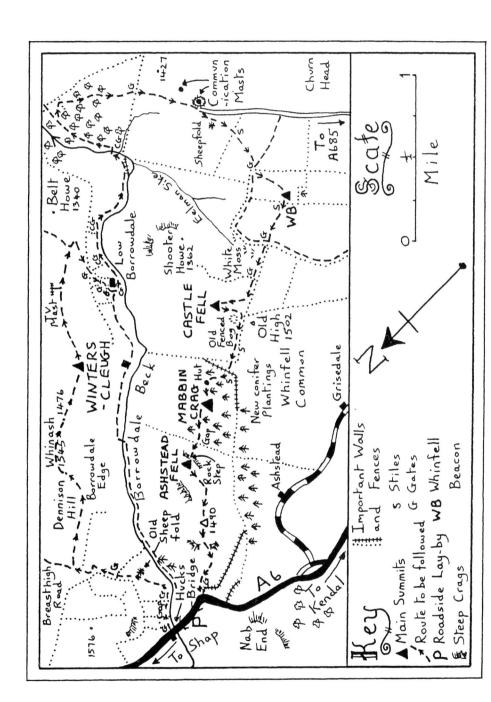

Key

- ⌖ Main Summits
- ⌁ Route to be followed
- P Roadside Lay-by WB Whinfell Beacon
- ▦ Important Walls and Fences
- S Stiles G Gates
- 🌿 Steep Crags

Scale

0 ¼ ½ ¾ 1 Mile

1427

Communication Masts

Churn Head

Sheepfold

To A685

Belt Howe 1340

T.V. Mast

Low Borrowdale

Eskman Sike

Shooter's Howe 1362

White Moss

WB

CASTLE FELL

Old Fenced Bog

Old High Whinfell 1502

Whinfell Common

Winters-Cleugh

Whinash 1343

Dennison Hill

Borrowdale Edge

Borrowdale Beck

Ashstead Fell

Mabbin Crag

Hut

Gap

Rock Step

1410

Old Sheep fold

New conifer Plantings

Grisedale

Ashstead

Breasthigh Road

1576

Hucks Bridge

A6

To Shap

Nab End

To Kendal

ROUTE DESCRIPTION

From the lay-by, head north along the A6 to cross Borrowdale Beck by Huck's Bridge. Immediately beyond, pass through a gate on the right and follow the beck on a grass track heading south east. After negotiating a wall gap and another gate, the rutted track swings left to mount the lower slopes of Borrowdale Edge adjacent to a fold.

Sheep in this valley home in on lone hikers, who assume the mantle of a pied piper, but only as far as the disintegrating fold. Beyond, the followers appear to sense that you are not after all the purveyor of tasty comestibles and so return to their pasture to accost other travellers. Their wait will doubtless be long as few people pass this way.

After a gate abutting what is enigmatically referred to as the Thunder Stone, climb alongside a wall for a short distance before this grooved trail named Breasthigh Road makes a sharp zig-zag prior to levelling out for the descent into Bretherdale. At the top of the pass, head right across windswept grassy hummocks over Dennison Hill and then in a wide left-hand arc onto the more notable hump of Whinash. Little more than a bump along the broad featureless ridge, it does not even have the temerity to sport a cairn.

Continue south east along the pathless wilderness, aiming for Winterscleugh a mile distant. Winterscleugh would count for nought if it were transported to Lakeland's Borrowdale, but here the merest hint of rocky outcrop assumes the significance of a desert oasis to nomadic herdsmen. There is little to detain us overlong, so head towards a prominent TV mast, which serves the viewing residents of Low Borrowdale.

Descend the verdant sheen to join a tractor route that merges with the main bridleway crossing from Roundthwaite. This bends abruptly right heading back towards the A6. When the in-take wall is reached, pass through a gate and drop down to the only inhabited settlement in Borrowdale.

Once through the farmyard, join the valley trail and head south east along the access road over two cattle grids. A substantial bridge is crossed after the beck veers north east, squeezing between pinched flanks that shelter and encourage the proliferation of oak woodland. Fork right up a clear track that meanders uphill through the woods before graduating across open moors in a south-westerly direction.

Beyond a wall gate, the communication mast should be passed with care. Head due west across undulating terrain through a wall stile. A direct line on a thinly marked trail will bring you to a gate at the wall corner where a farm track circumvents Whinfell Beacon.

Through the gate, make your way up the grassy sward to the top of the Beacon. An ancient storm-lashed signal flare site dating back to the 15th century, it has now been superseded by the steel towers below. A stile gives access to the west side of the summit wall, after which a leisurely descent brings you to the surrounding wall. Follow another through two gates then bear right to climb Castle Fell.

Rejoin the wall and accompany it to a corner where a stile is crossed. The first swathe of baby conifers is reached after another 50 yards, together with a fence stile. Thereafter, the tortuous trail passes through virgin forest by an abandoned shepherd's hut beyond which a short pull gives onto the top of Mabbin Crag. There follows a wide swing to the right down through more plantings, which lead to a gap in the cross-fell wall. Beyond here, mount a six-foot rock step, the last obstacle before the ascent of the three hills that make up Ashstead Fell.

Overlooking the main road, the final cairn is often falsely regarded as the true summit. Carry on down a clear path to meet the A6, followed by a short road walk back to the lay-by.

15. UP THE SPOUT

Start and Finish: Plenty of parking space is available on the left verge of Fairmile Road immediately south of Carlingill Bridge.

Summits Climbed:	Docker Knott	— 1723 feet
	Fell Head	— 2080 feet
	Linghaw	— 1625 feet

Total Height Climbed: 1600 feet

Distance Walked: 6 miles

Nearest Centre: Tebay

Map Required: Ordnance Survey Pathfinder Series 1:25000, Sedbergh & Baugh Fell sheet SD 69/79

INTRODUCTION

The first half of this walk follows the north-west boundary of the Yorkshire Dales National Park. On the ground there is no indication of such as we accompany Carlingill Beck into the core of the Howgill Massif. The reasoning that dictated the course of the park boundary through the middle of these smooth-skinned behemoths remains a mystery.

The impressive cutting of Carlin Gill hides one of the most specacular gorges in northern England, a mind-boggling attraction that makes the Howgills a firm favourite with me at least. Gladiatorial forces of nature have battled to produce a magnificent waterfall second only in its awesome power to the mighty Dungeon Ghyll of Great Langdale.

73

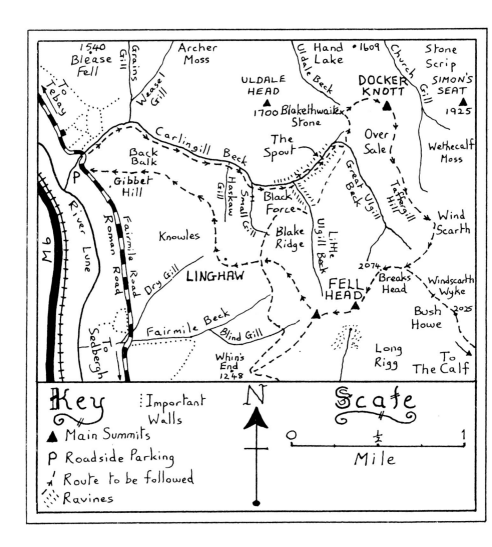

1540
Blease
Fell

Grains Gill

Archer
Moss

• 1609

Hand
Lake

Church Gill

Stone
Scrip

SIMON'S
SEAT

1925

To Tebay

Wease Gill

ULDALE
HEAD

Uldale Beck

DOCKER
KNOTT

Over
Sale

Wethecalf
Moss

1700 Blakethwaite
Stone

Carlingill Beck

The
Spout

Back
Balk

P

Gibbet
Hill

Haskaw Gill

Small Gill

Black
Force

Great Ugill Beck

Taffers Gill
Hill

Wind
Scarth

Knowles

Blake
Ridge

Little
Ugill Beck

River Lune

Roman Road

Fairmile Road

Dry Gill

LINGHAW

M 6

2074

FELL
HEAD

Breaks
Head

Windscarth
Wyke

2025

To Sedbergh

Fairmile Beck

Blind Gill

Bush
Howe

Whin's
End
1248

Long
Rigg

To
The Calf

To Tebay

Key

⋮ Important
Walls

▲ Main Summits

P Roadside Parking

↗ Route to be followed

∴ Ravines

N

Scale

0   ½   1

Mile

74

Few walks that venture onto high ground can avoid man-made inter-ference such as walls and fences. Yet on this circuit, no such barriers to progress were encountered at any stage. Although handy as guides to direction finding in mist, any hindrance to free movement across the fells is anathema to all who love to wander at will across unspoilt terrain.

ROUTE DESCRIPTION

From Carlingill Bridge, accompany the beck on its right bank along a thin path, which sticks close to the valley floor but above the level of the flood plain. Between the steep flanks, the stream meanders across river benches

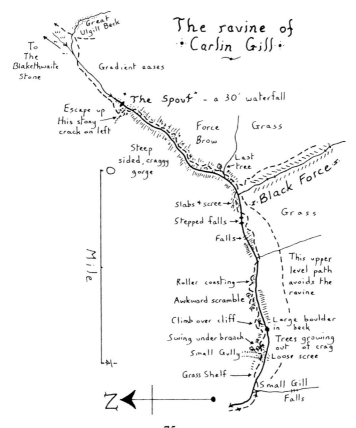

75

from previous inundations. This deep gash in the western phalanx eventually narrows to form the cataclysmic ravine of Force Brow.

As you move steadily upstream, the anticipation of better things to come grows rapidly. Beyond the falls of Small Gill, it becomes necessary to utilise the bed of the watercourse, criss-crossing from side to side as the water level dictates. In periods of high rainfall when the power and volume increases dramatically, you may find it impossible to make further progress. Drier conditions are, therefore, recommended in order to take full advantage of the delights on offer.

After the initial taster, the open wound of Black Force is exposed in all its sinister glory; a precipitous ravine of shattered rock, it can be investigated if further progress up Carlin Gill is judged to be unwise. These inspiring and grandiose surroundings are hidden from casual view and only seek to confirm the opinion that the Howgills have a powerful magnetism entirely their own.

All being well, continue up the rock-strewn gorge sticking close to the chattering beck for superior sport until you arrive at The Spout. This plunging cataract closely rivals its more eminent counterpart at Cautley on the eastern fringe but is infinitely preferable, being secluded and largely unknown. Escape a soaking by climbing up the grassy left bank, thence returning to the stream and an easier gradient.

Soon thereafter, the main beck is seen to swing sharply south west debouching from the upper reaches of Breaks. At this point, join a clear track coming in from the right. This directs you to the amphitheatre marked by the diminutive Blakethwaite Stone, a watershed between north and south drainage. Ascend the short but steep eastern slope, bearing right onto the compact grass top of Docker Knott, which is surmounted by a cairn of miniscule proportions.

Head south around the left hem of Over Sale, aiming for a clear path that ascends the broad ridge of Taffergill Hill. The path fades as Wind Scarth is neared but another is soon joined, bearing right to merge with the principal circuit of the Howgills at Breaks Head. This major footway from The Calf heads south west onto the summit of Fell Head, easily distinguished from afar by its own integral flag pole. The subsidiary top is slightly lower and adrift from the main route.

From this latter eminence, the whole expanse of the Lune Gorge is laid out below. A vibrant gap in the northern fells, it has stimulated the flow of traffic since Roman times. The constant motorway hum does nought, however, to dispel the magic of this landscape, which draws me back time and again.

Head north down Blake Ridge on a faint path, bearing left to cross a narrow col and up the facing slope onto Linghaw. The broad featureless sward has no recognisable summit worth mentioning in view of the dearth of rocks needed for construction purposes. Maintain a north-west course above Carlin Gill, picking up a clear trail over Back Balk. Don't panic at the presence of numerous rough-looking fell ponies. They are herbivores and unlikely to regard you as a tasty morsel.

Pass to the right of Gibbet Hill where human bones have been unearthed, no doubt the remains of sheep rustlers who were cursorily disposed of in the appropriate fashion of a by-gone era. A brief stroll down Fairmile Road will return you to the car.

16. THE EDGE OF NEWLANDS

Start and Finish: A quarter of a mile south west of Little Town is located a car park abutting Newlands Beck at Chapel Bridge.

Summits Climbed:	Dale Head	— 2473 feet
	Hindscarth	— 2385 feet
	Robinson	— 2417 feet

Total Height Climbed: 2800 feet

Distance Walked: 9½ miles

Nearest Centre: Seatoller/Buttermere

Map Required: Ordnance Survey English Lakes 1:25000, North West area sheet

INTRODUCTION

Newlands is renowned for the rich veins of copper ore that were mined by German immigrants working under royal patronage from the 17th century. Lead and silver were also obtained from the lonely fells, which encouraged continuous operation for over 400 years and played a vital role in transforming Keswick into a prosperous industrial community.

In Upper Newlands, two of the most productive mines in north Lakeland (Dale Head, and Goldscope — German for God's Gift) were empowered by the Company of Mines Royal in 1565 to ' . . . search, dig, try, roast and melt all manner of mines and ores . . . ', the Crown in the form of the first Elizabeth graciously accepting ten per cent of the precious metal profits. Such a mercenary attitude towards the environment in the present climate of rural conservation would see an army of protectionists grabbing for their injunction writs. The map overleaf indicates the main areas of industrial endeavour in the Lake District.

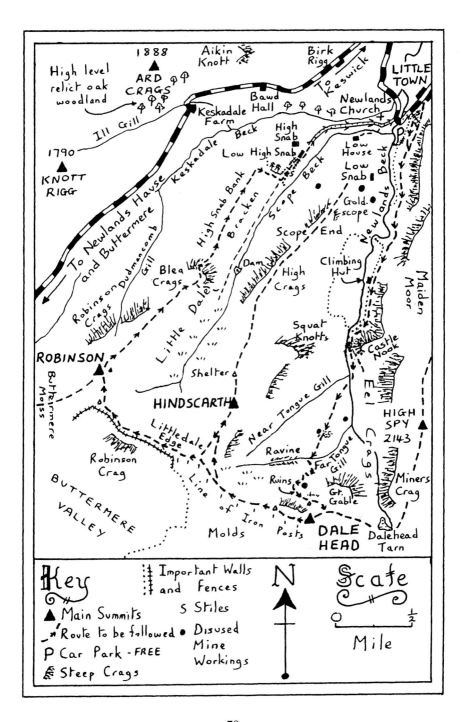

High level relict oak woodland

1888

Aikin Knott

Birk Rigg

LITTLE TOWN

ARD CRAGS

To Keswick

Bawd Hall

Newlands Church

Keskadale Farm

Keskadale Beck

High Snab

Ill Gill

Low High Snab

Low House

Low Snab

1790

KNOTT RIGG

To Newlands Hause and Buttermere

High Snab Bank

Bracken

Scope Beck

Gold-scope

Scope End

Newlands Beck

Robinson Dudmancomb Gill

Blea Crags

Dam

High Crags

Climbing Hut

Maiden Moor

Little Dale

Squat Knotts

Castle Nook

ROBINSON

Shelter

HINDSCARTH

Eel Crags

HIGH SPY 2143

Buttermere Moss

Littledale Edge

Near Tongue Gill

Ravine

Far Tongue Gill

Robinson Crag

BUTTERMERE VALLEY

Line of Iron

Molds

Posts

Ruins

Gt. Gable

DALE HEAD

Miners Crag

Dalehead Tarn

Key

Important Walls and Fences

S Stiles

▲ Main Summits

Route to be followed

● Disused Mine Workings

P Car Park - FREE

Steep Crags

N

Scale

0   ½

Mile

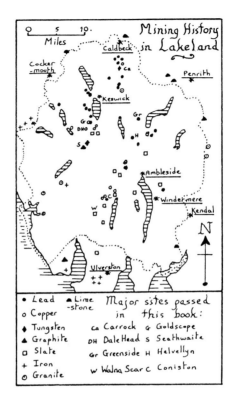

Today, in Newlands, the spoil tips and disused levels of these once-thriving mines remain desolate and solitary. But they do provide a lasting memorial to the burrowing tenacity of our forefathers deep within the heart of mountain Lakeland.

ROUTE DESCRIPTION

Return towards Little Town, keeping a look-out for a fence stile on the right. Head south on a grass trod, which soon merges with the principal gravel track originally constructed to service the mines at the valley head. Only passing fell trekkers and farmers, together with mountain men tarrying at the climbing hut, make use of it today, although the ghostly presence of tramping miners is never far removed in the heavily-charged atmosphere.

Continue down the flat valley floor, noting the symmetrical tips of the Goldscope Mine on the western slope below Scope End. This most eminent of mines began life way back in the 13th century when a nine-foot copper vein was discovered; an auspicious start to a love affair with metallica, finally culminating with lead extraction during the Victorian era.

Work around the gnarled elbow of Castle Nook, striding between further mounds of detritus, into the upper valley. Ahead, a linear groove slanting up the opposite grass slope indicates the course to follow. Cross Newlands Beck, making effective use of resident boulders, skilful selection of a suitable route being essential when the waters are in spate if boot inundation is to be avoided. Climb the verdant bank, keeping to the left of the conduit until a patch of shaft tailings is crossed.

Take a rest here to marvel at the dragon's teeth of Eel Crags snarling defiantly on the east façade below High Spy. The path continues straight ahead on a shelf before negotiating the rock-strewn ravine of Far Tongue Gill. Thereafter, it pursues a zig-zag course up into the hollow occupied by the skeletal remains of Dale Head Mine where streaks of bright green malachite add a splash of colour to the otherwise sombre prison-grey surroundings.

Note a thin yet clear trail picking a delicate path above the massive buttress of Great Gable. Not quite of the aristocratic grandeur of the other more celebrated leviathan, it presents no less a precipitous crag, which needs careful footage. This north face of Dale Head demands total concentration in icy conditions but still remains an inspiring and lofty traverse. Bear right on easier ground to gain the summit cairn.

From here, head east along Hindscarth Edge on a sound ridge path accompanied by a row of intermittent iron posts. Bear right as the Hindscarth Massif is approached to follow a northerly course across the gently-shelving swell onto the main fell. The broad plateau of Hindscarth is unusual in that it stands proud from the main ridge system and thus requires a detour of half a mile if the gravelly summit is to be visited. But it is to the abruptly soaring north ridge that the fell owes its principal attraction.

To reach Robinson, it is necessary to circumvent Little Dale by retracing your steps to regain the Edge. Cross the deep grass depression of Littledale Edge and climb the opposite slope alongside a wire fence. When it swings away left, head due north across the intervening plateau to gain the summit formed into parallel blades of jagged outcropping.

Thereafter, our way lies north east across easy ground, which becomes increasingly steep above the hidden bluff of Robinson Crags. Blea Crags need special care in bad conditions in order to descend the rock stairway in safety. A pleasant stroll along High Snab Bank culminates in a sharp right down a foot-stepped grass ladder to valley level.

Make a left into a walled lane, crossing a stile to pass by the illogically lyrical Low High Snab. Beyond the farm buildings, the lane becomes metalled and should be followed past Newlands Church back to the car park.

17. HOWGILL EXPERIENCE

Start and Finish: The farming hamlet of Longdale provides ample parking space and you would be unlucky indeed to find others there of similar notion.

Summits Climbed:		
	Langdale Knott	— 1560 feet
	The Calf	— 2220 feet
	Docker Knott	— 1723 feet

Total Height Climbed: 2000 feet

Distance Walked: 13 miles

Nearest Centre: Tebay

Maps Required: Ordnance Survey Pathfinder Series 1:25000, Tebay & Kirkby Stephen sheet NY 60/70, Sedbergh & Baugh Fell sheet SD 69/79

INTRODUCTION

There can be few more exhilarating tracts of upland than the Howgills and in fine weather the fells provide hiking that is second to none. The Calf rises but little above the surrounding ridge tops yet never fails to attract fell wanderers like bees to a honeypot.

For those who love to stride out over gently shelving terrain, where miles are quickly devoured, the Howgills remain a remote fastness incomparable in their rustic charm. You rapidly become absorbed into the unspoilt landscape which the tourist invasion has thankfully ignored.

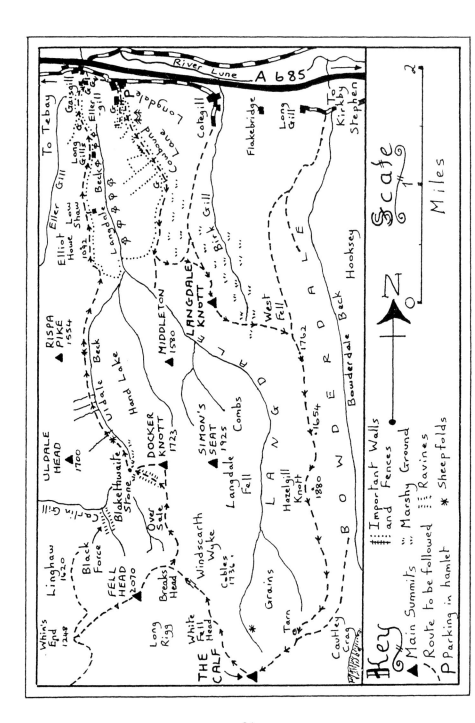

Key

▲ Main Summits
∴ Route to be followed
P Parking in hamlet
⫶⫶ Important Walls and Fences
‹‹ Marshy Ground
⫶⫶⫶ Ravines
✳ Sheepfolds

Scale

N

0   1   2
Miles

This splendid isolation is only disturbed by the sound of chattering becks and birdsong. In spring, new-born lambs add their bleating to this chorus. No motor roads penetrate any of the deep valleys, which adds to the sense of seclusion, and hikers are able to step back rapidly in time to a world of rare tranquillity. Long summer days allow you to appreciate fully the true nature of this El Dorado, there to venture forth alone and unmolested by the trappings of modern civilisation.

ROUTE DESCRIPTION

Head south past a row of cottages, taking a left through a gate to enter Cowbound Lane. This grassy walled track connects the hamlet of Longdale with the open fell. After a sharp right, the track follows a dead straight course south east. Beyond a small conifer plantation, the right wall veers away. Continue ahead for a quarter of a mile, after which the route becomes fully walled again.

At the end of the lane, a gate gives access to open ground. Keep right on a strong track alongside the final in-take wall, marching south. Where it forks down into Langdale, slant left on a thin track, which strengthens across grassy mossland. As this trail swings left, maintain a straight course on a south-easterly bearing to meet the up-coming track from Cotegill. The summit of Langdale Knott is soon reached. A verdant sward guarded by a platoon of sheep, it is devoid of all stony matter save for the ten (yes, I counted them) small rocks brought to the top by kind-hearted souls wishing to make their own little contribution towards a cairn on this otherwise undistinguished mound.

Continue down the shoulder, bearing east to negotiate the marshy depression of Birkgill Moss. Thereafter, a simple uphill plod brings you to the broad ridge of West Fell. The easy south-bound trail provides a scintillating high-level means of attaining The Calf. Undulating and without any notable landmarks, this is a ridge walk for clear conditions when the surrounding fell systems can be identified and the true splendour of landscape relished to the full. Climbing is gradual and hardly likely to set your heart muscles a'quivering.

The ridge slices through half the Howgill Massif dividing the deep, penetrative valleys of Bowderdale and Langdale. At its head, it merges into the summit plateau, which marks the northern boundary of the Yorkshire Dales National Park. A distinct path rises south west past a small tarn. Follow this to gain the white trig column atop The Calf before edging north west around the rim of the watershed.

Only on the substantial descent to the exquisitely neat depression of Windscarth Wyke does the summit disappear from view. A sharp ascent of the facing slope brings us to Breaks Head and a parting from the established route. Bear right down Windscarth Ridge for a quarter-mile where the path swings abruptly left over Taffergill Hill. A mile-long stroll on a thin grass trod topping Over Sale leads to Docker Knott.

For those of you who have not already ticked it off, coast ahead then change down into second gear for the facing bank. Then head west from the cairn down into Blakethwaite Bottom to meet the rest of us who have swung left into a deep unnamed cutting, which leads directly to the pass and the celebrated 'Stone'. In the Lake District, this insignificant rock would remain unnoticed as just another one among many, but here it assumes gargantuan proportions where such landmarks are revered, and even eulogised by mapmakers.

After paying due homage, follow a distinct path along the valley floor of Uldale Beck, a fine example of a water-cut dale rising steeply on either flank. The path sticks closely to the beck but at the second sheepfold, begins to climb gradually out of the valley on a well-graded course to meet the up-coming in-take wall at Uldale End. The track follows the walled ridge over Elliott Howe between the Ellergill and Langdale valleys.

Stick with the track as it becomes the access road for Low Shaw Farm and leads all the way down to the farming hamlet of Ellergill. The road becomes hemmed into a wide walled causeway. Bear right through a farmyard to gain the side road back to Longdale.

18. WEST OF THE DUDDON

Start and Finish: Pull off the fell road to the west of Ulpha Park at Low Craghall to park by a stile on the right at grid reference 182915.

Summits Climbed:	Whitfell	— 1876 feet
	Stainton Pike	— 1632 feet
	Hesk Fell	— 1566 feet
	The Pike	— 1214 feet

Total Height Climbed:	1800 feet
Distance Walked:	8½ miles
Nearest Centre:	Ulpha
Map Required:	Ordnance Survey English Lakes 1:25000, South West area sheet

INTRODUCTION

Whenever anybody asks for my opinion as to the most remote and least known corner of the Lake District, I have no hesitation in suggesting the fell country west of the Duddon Valley. Totally unspoilt and rarely visited, the rolling uplands display a subdued appearance more akin to Pennine moors than the glacial topography normally associated with Lakeland. Yet this landscape remains firmly entrenched within the boundaries of the National Park.

Whilst the vast majority of hikers continue to scour out the central core, providing endless work for the footpath rebuilders, the bleak wilderness north of Black Combe attracts only those seeking solitude. Never have I encountered a human soul once the lower in-take fields are left behind.

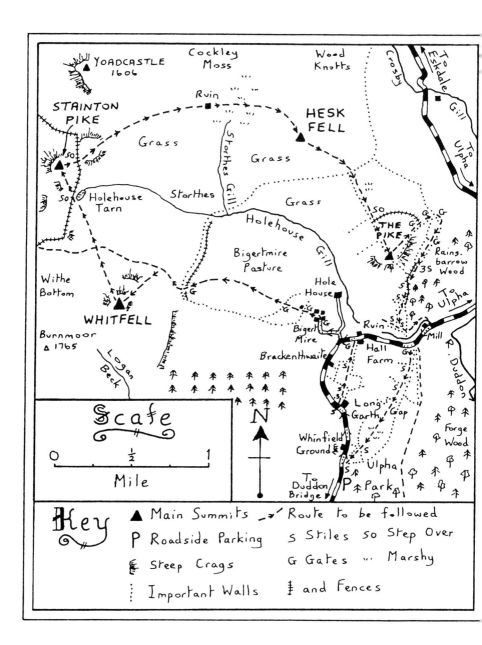

YOADCASTLE 1606

Cockley Moss

Wood Knotts

Crosby

To Eskdale

Gill

To Ulpha

STAINTON PIKE

Ruin

HESK FELL

Grass

Storthes Gill

Grass

Grass

SO

Storthes

Holehouse Tarn

THE PIKE

Rains. barrow Wood

Holehouse Gill

Withe Bottom

Bigertmire Pasture

3S

Hole House

To Ulpha

WHITFELL

Ruin

Mill

Burnmoor △ 1765

Logan Beck

Bigert Mire

Hall Farm

R. Duddon

Brackenthwaite

Forge Wood

Long Garth

Gap

Whinfield Ground

Ulpha Park

To Duddon Bridge

P

Scafe

0   ½   1

Mile

N

Key

▲ Main Summits   �ି Route to be followed

P Roadside Parking   s Stiles   so Step Over

⸕ Steep Crags   G Gates   ⠒ Marshy

⋮ Important Walls   ‡ and Fences

88

Paths are virtually non-existent and even the lone east-west bridleway is difficult to follow for much of its course. Clear weather conditions are, therefore, a must. There is no joy in labouring across acres of tussocky moorland enclosed within a nebulous grey mantle. On the day of my most recent visit, the high fells to the north lay shrouded beneath a woolly blanket whilst this remote backwater luxuriated under a warm if somewhat diluted blue sky.

Only the extremities of this south-west enclave witness the passage of human traffic. Harter Fell with its frost-shattered pyramid shape contrasts markedly with the sleek dome of Black Combe. Between the two, isolated crusty outcrops poke above the lonely grass swathe, ignored and largely untouched.

ROUTE DESCRIPTION

Head north along the fell road as far as Long Garth. Take the footpath immediately beyond the farm access gate over a stile. Cross the fields by means of three other stiles to reach Old Hall Farm and so rejoin the fell road. Turn left up the road past the old hall ruins, bearing right and immediately left to follow the access road bound for Bigert Mire. Beyond this unusual cluster of farm cottages, take the bridleway north west to gain the open fell after two more gates.

The clear trail fades across Bigertmire Pasture, making a wide left-hand sweep westwards to a fence, which has replaced the disintegrating wall. Pass through a gate, continuing along the track for 200 yards, before forking left to head south west up an easy slope onto Whitfell. Beyond the flat summit, an ancient tumulus holds sway and is surmounted by a substantial cairn.

Head north-north-west down the gentle northern flank of the fell, crossing the faint bridleway to take advantage of a clear path bound for Holehouse Tarn. To gain access to Stainton Pike, a wire fence must be crossed. Those with long legs will experience no difficulties; others of a more diminutive stature should take heed of their nether regions.

After a visit to this fine summit, recross the fence north of the tarn to pursue a tortuous course through low crags. Thereafter, a wide swing around the source of Storthes Gill takes us east towards Hesk Fell. At the watershed, a ruined shepherd's hut is passed, clearly what must have been one of the loneliest duties in Lakeland. Cross the marshy depression and climb the north slope of Hesk Fell to reach the minute summit cairn.

There is nothing here to encourage one to tarry, so descend the slope, aiming south west for a gate in the in-take wall. Through this, accompany the wall on your right up onto the splendid rocky top properly referred to as The Pike. The wall crosses the actual summit, which provides a panoramic vista over the Duddon Valley to the east. Here is a peak of some renown, which is at least deserving of a cairn. Perhaps some enterprising individual could rectify this omission.

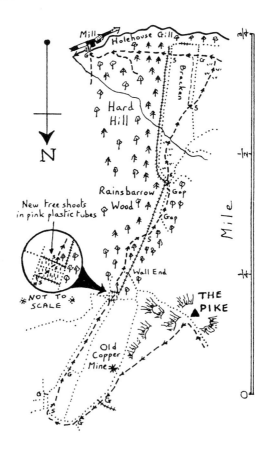

To reach Rainsbarrow Wood, it is necessary to detour north east, following a wall that allows passage through three gates, before swinging sharply back on itself to enter the wood a mere 450 feet below The Pike. Cross a series of stiles to accompany a fence along the western edge of the wood before exiting via a wall stile.

Head south along a wall down an easy grass bank until a clear path is reached above the ravine occupied by Holehouse Gill. From here, bear left along the path to re-enter Rainsbarrow Wood, proceeding downhill to gain the fell road over a bridge close to an old mill. Turn right past the chimney and climb the steep road as far as Millbrow. Choose the second right of way on your left through a gate. Follow the wall to a stile; thereafter veer right away from the wall to mount another across the field.

Pass a small copse on your right through a wall gap, after which the path fades. Maintain a south-westerly course over another stile, aiming for the signpost ahead and your car. In view of the remote terrain covered on this walk, the distance is further than might be expected. Do not underestimate the challenge offered.

19. ABOVE THE SWALE

Start and Finish: Open road parking is available above the hamlet of Ivelet en route to Gunnerside and adjacent to the start of the old mine road at GR 941983.

Summit Climbed:	Rogan's Seat — 2203 feet
Total Height Climbed:	1400 feet
Distance Walked:	10½ miles
Nearest Centre:	Muker
Map Required:	Ordnance Survey Yorkshire Dales 1:25000, Northern and Central area sheet

INTRODUCTION

A brief scan of the area on the Ordnance Survey map sandwiched between the River Swale and Gunnerside Gill is sufficient to indicate the presence in large numbers of that illustrious yet much maligned grouse. This vast open tract of heather-clad moorland to the north of Muker acts as a temporary breeding ground for these sleek, sought-after game birds. Butts and shooting boxes abound. If you are an ardent hiker and, like me, do not yet wish to join our feathered friends in that great aviary in the sky, then the 'Glorious 12th' (of August) should be a date to give this otherwise splendid tramp a decisive thumbs down.

Before grouse were commercially bred here, the mining of lead brought wealth and employment to the valley until well into the 19th century. Buildings and spoil heaps are much in evidence in the deep trench of Gunnerside Gill, which cuts a deep furrow across the surrounding bleak wilderness.

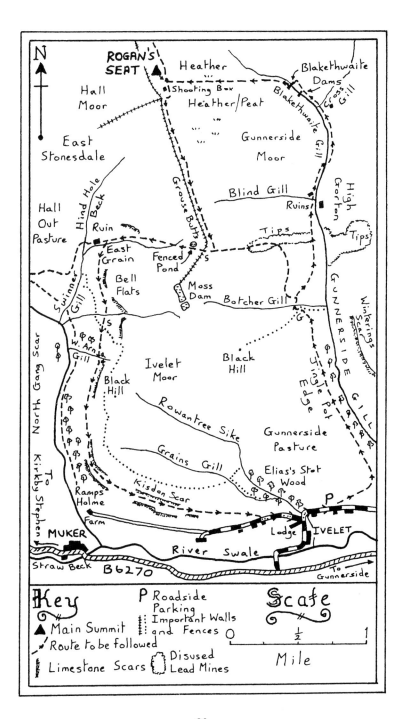

N

ROGAN'S SEAT ▲

Heather

Blakethwaite Dams

Shooting Box

Blakethwaite Gill

Cross Gill

Hall Moor

Heather/Peat

East Stonesdale

Gunnerside Moor

Hind Hole Beck

Blind Gill

High Gorton

Ruins

Hall Out Pasture

Ruin

Grouse Butts

Tips

Tips

East Grain

Fenced Pond

S

Swinner Gill

Bell Flats

Moss Dam

Botcher Gill

G

GUNNERSIDE GILL

S

W. Arn Gill

Winterings Scars

North Gang Scar

Black Hill

Ivelet Moor

Black Hill

Jingle Pot Edge

Rowantree Sike

Gunnerside Pasture

To Kirkby Stephen

Grains Grill

Elias's Stot Wood

Ramps Holme Farm

Kisdon Scar

P

MUKER

Lodge

IVELET

River Swale

Straw Beck

B6270

To Gunnerside

Key

⌇
▲ Main Summit
⌇ Route to be followed
⌇ Limestone Scars

P Roadside Parking
⌇ Important Walls and Fences
⬡ Disused Lead Mines

Scale

0 ½ 1

Mile

In days long since confined to the history books, miners had to walk many miles to their work and often knitted scarves to pass the time. 'Let's sit down for six needles' became an oft-quoted utterance from those in need of a rest. But many were not sad to see the demise of this industrial phase in Swaledale's past. Local graveyards are full of the remains of young men cut off in their prime by the scourge of lead poisoning.

Today, the strategic town of Richmond guards the eastern entrance to the dale, yet the most picturesque and photographed award must go to Muker, which lies towards the headwaters of the Swale. This 'cultivated enclosure' is a Norse settlement sited on Neolithic foundations and is the first substantial Dales village encountered by those of us travelling from the western counties. Overshadowed by scarred edges of weathered limestone, it is little wonder that many visitors travel no further. Our way however leads on to the parking at Dykes Head above Ivelet.

ROUTE DESCRIPTION

Take the rough mine road slanting north east across the open fell, which swings north into the enclosed confines of Gunnerside Gill. The track maintains a level course under Jingle Pot Edge before curving left into the side valley of Botcher Gill. Beyond a wall gate, the gill is crossed by means of a substantial bridge.

At this point, the main gravel road is abandoned in favour of a right fork along a less obvious grass path, which continues along the valley flank past Lownathwaite mines. Cross the lower reaches of the lead hush and descend to the valley floor, where the tributary of Blind Gill swells the surging torrent of the main beck. Ancient shells of abandoned mine buildings are ample evidence of serious industrial enterprise. Where natural resources abound, Man will do his utmost to wrest them from the land whatever the environmental consequences — if not for national prosperity, then certainly to feed hungry mouths. So who are we to complain of such necessary endeavour?

At this point, the valley sides close in. After a further quarter-mile, cross the watercourse to proceed upstream bound for the dual dams of

Blakethwaite. Both have been breached by the continuous buffeting of powerful torrents of water and should be negotiated with care. Make your way up to the higher dam and then cross to the west bank for the climb out of the broadening dale head. No paths are in evidence and the tussocky heather-clad moors make progress on this section slow and tiring. Maintain a westerly bearing, which should be strictly adhered to in misty conditions, across the featureless peat hags in order to gain the fell track without mishap. This rough highway has been specially constructed for the benefit of 'grouse lovers'.

Cross the undulating expanse of Gunnerside Moor. Avoid stepping on the many nests that lie concealed amidst the heathery carpet. On your approach, parent birds can often be seen assiduously beating the ground with their wings to warn their infant offspring that the dreaded *homo erectus* is close by, an effective tactic aimed at encouraging immediate flight.

Turn right along the track for a quarter of a mile to attain the high point of Rogan's Seat, which is an obvious raised plinth surmounting the summit plateau. Hardy Swaledale sheep with black heads and legs will assuredly try to eject you from their inherited domain.

From Rogan's Seat, rejoin the trail and head south-south-east for one-and-a-half miles until it veers to the east. Take a right here on a clear grass path, then cross over a fence stile. Leave this distinct route to follow a more interesting descent of East Grain, which becomes steeper and rougher as height is lost. Watch out for a thin trail on the opposite bank immediately abutting some old mine ruins.

Accompany this out of the confines of Swinner Gill, swinging south along the terrace route into the upper valley of the Swale. After a wall stile, the following two miles follow a truly delightful course along the steep scarred flanks below Ivelet Moor. Every step is a joy to walk. Take time out to appreciate fully its firm underlying foundation as the path meanders through wonderful scenery.

Beyond a deviation into the stony gully of West Arn Gill, the way passes through a linear 'conurbation' of rabbit warrens, the like of which I have never previously encountered.

Once Kisdon Scar is passed, the indistinct path gradually descends and heads east above Muker, eventually merging with a metalled access road from Ramps Holme Farm. Stick with this past Gunnerside Lodge, bending sharp left and down over Grains Gill before climbing back up the open road for a further quarter-mile to Dyke Heads.

20. BOARDALE BONANZA

Start and Finish: There is plenty of roadside parking on the Boardale access road just to the north of Garth Heads.

Summits Climbed:

Place Fell	— 2154 feet
Angletarn Pikes	— 1857 feet
Beda Head	— 1664 feet

Total Height Climbed: 2550 feet

Distance Walked: 7½ miles

Nearest Centre: Pooley Bridge

Map Required: Ordnance Survey English Lakes 1:25000, North East area sheet

INTRODUCTION

There can be few more delightful valleys in Lakeland than the secluded Boardale. A little over two miles in length, it remains a backwater that few have ever heard of, let alone visited. Yet here is presented the authentic flavour of a by-gone age where the interfering hand of progress has passed on.

Approaching from Pooley Bridge, Hallin Fell, the guardian of Martindale Common, attempts to make life difficult for the unwary motorist by standing in the way of direct access to the glens beyond. The sharp hairpin ascent to The Hause stimulates the adrenalin such that only tenacious bulldogs will persevere to the extremeties.

Around the northern shoulder of Beda Fell, one enters a time warp untouched by the passing fancies of contemporary man. Once the array of valley in-takes have been negotiated, no further barriers to onward movement will be encountered.

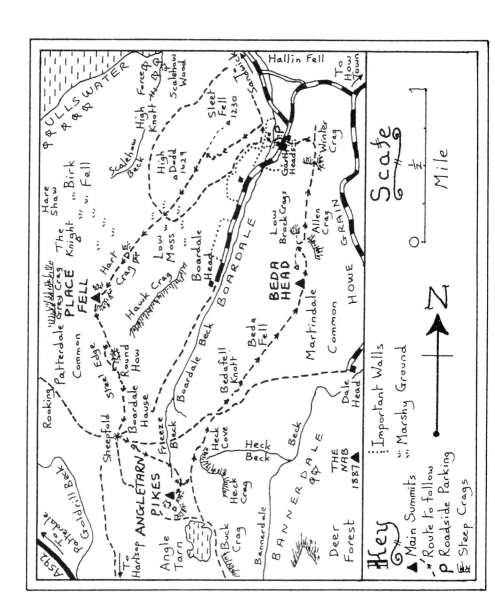

Key

▲ Main Summits
↗ Route to follow
P Roadside Parking
⛰ Steep Crags
⋯ Important Walls
„ Marshy Ground

N

Scale

0 ···· ½ ···· 1

Mile

It is unfortunate that the authorities felt the need to erect yellow trail markers on the lower access paths when proper use of the 2½ inch map is sufficient indication of the right of way. The skills associated with fell walking should be encouraged so that only those who have bothered to master the techniques can venture into terrain that is stunningly beautiful whilst retaining an inherent danger that must never be underestimated.

ROUTE DESCRIPTION

To avoid any confusion on the initial phase of this walk, use should be made of the large-scale map encompassing the in-bye fields abutting Garth Heads. Walking south towards Boardale Head, take a right down a walled track. After a stile the path bears left, leaving the confines of the wall to cross Boardale Beck at a ford. If wellies are the preferred footwear, then strike merrily across. Wisely-booted individuals are catered for 20 yards upstream where a stone foot bridge allows dry passage to the far bank.

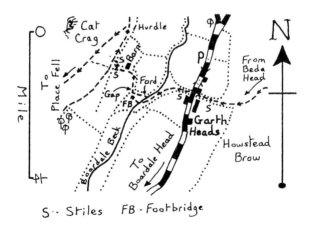

S ·· Stiles   FB - Footbridge

Ignore the route of a permissive footpath to fork right across a marshy tract, rejoining the main right-of-way, which passes left of a barn up to a double stile ahead. Over the final in-take wall, head right beside it as far as a hurdle in the accompanying wall. Make a sharp left here to join a well-graded bench way that slants obliquely across the steep south-east flank of Sleet Fell.

Climbing above the valley floor provides intimate views of the textbook sculpting of a fine glacial trough. After a couple of zig-zags, the first of which squeezes through a deep rock groove, the trail eases to pass left of High Dodd, a secondary summit along the northern arm of Place Fell. Continuing ahead in a south-westerly direction, we cross the swampy amphitheatre of Low Moss, maintaining a straight course towards the craggy heights above.

What appears as the final haul turns out to be a cairned outlier known as Hart Crag. The high point of our hike lies a third of a mile to the south west across easy terrain, which culminates in an exhilarating scramble to the top of Place Fell. To the west, the Helvellyn range is displayed in all its splendour.

Of those who walk in Patterdale, few can resist an ascent of Place Fell, and the climb via Boardale Hause is the most popular route. In fine weather and especially on Sundays, rambling clubs galore make for the dizzy heights above, so be prepared for the customary 'nodding donkey' syndrome on the descent to the Hause. Thereafter all is peace, quiet and solitude once again.

Keep left of a prominent sheepfold in the pass, slanting up to join the bridleway bound for Bannerdale. After no more than 100 yards, an obvious cairn marks the divergence of a thin trod in the grass, which aims south east towards Angletarn Pikes. Cross the shallow depression of Freeze Beck and mount the easy slope beyond to reach a solid cairn on the lip of the undulating plateau.

Bear right here to climb the nobbly spine onto the highest Pike. Its twin lies 200 yards to the south east. Few people bother to come this way, so your lunch is unlikely to be disturbed. Now is the time to wallow in the role of king of the castle before returning down the gentle spine to bear right across the rolling landscape. Make for the ridge path a third of a mile east, then head north towards Beda Fell.

An easy unhindered lope lies before you along a delightful route, which crosses the Bannerdale highway just prior to mounting the rocky tor of Bedafell Knott. Descending Bedafell Knott, a gentle incline on grass is soon eaten up and Beda Head top gained. This is a fine roost for contemplation.

Head down the north shoulder but beware of a red herring above Raven Crag. So watch for an abrupt right swing, which safely carries you round the crusty outlier ahead. Continue on over Winter Crag, after which a grass path swings left off the ridge to descend steeply to Garth Heads. A gap in the in-take wall allows access to the valley road beyond a fence stile and re-entry to the push-button age of the late 20th century.

21. AROUND BANNISDALE

Start and Finish: Heading north on the A6 from Kendal, turn left down a side road 200 yards before Bannisdale Low Bridge at GR 541010. Various pull-ins are available.

Summits Climbed:	Whiteside Pike	— 1302 feet
	Capplebarrow	— 1683 feet
	Swinklebank	— 1819 feet
	White Howe	— 1737 feet

Total Height Climbed: 2000 feet

Distance Walked: 10½ miles

Nearest Centre: Kendal

Map Required: Ordnance Survey English Lakes 1:25000, South East area sheet

INTRODUCTION

Even on a fine bank holiday when you would expect no corner of Lakeland to be overlooked by invading hordes of tourists, the secluded valley of Bannisdale and its surrounding ridges is unlikely to disappoint. But where, you may well ask, is Bannisdale? One of a series of parallel dales in the south-east corner of the District, its undulating terrain remains the preserve of avid felltrekkers who delight in their own company. Make no mistake, however, the way is long and much of it is pathless, as one would expect along ridges where even the celebrated Herdwicks are in short supply.

This territory has little in common with the rugged heartland of the Lake District and is more akin to the extensive moorlands associated with Pennine walking. Once the rocky oasis of Whiteside Pike is left behind, all is grass

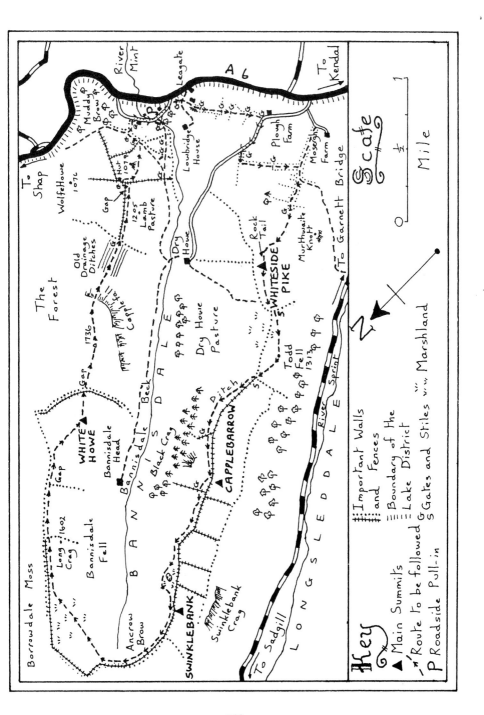

Key

▲ Main Summits
↗ Route to be followed
G Gates and Stiles
P Roadside Pull-in

ⅲⅲ Important Walls and Fences
☰ Boundary of the Lake District
ₜ v/v Marshland

Scale

0   ½   1
Mile

103

and exposed outcrops are a rare sight. Striding out along the gently-shelving backbone provides an exhilarating tonic for the troubled mind where petty irritations are put into their true perspective.

Here is untamed wilderness where the hand of Man has wrought little change over the centuries. Let us hope that such valleys remain unsullied by the 'progress' that much of our National Park has been subjected to in recent years. Although on the outer fringes, Bannisdale lies at the heart of all that is precious in the Lake District.

ROUTE DESCRIPTION

Fifty yards down the side road from the A6, take a bridleway on the left. Cross the broad access track from Lowbridge House to climb left of a small copse. The path continues on grass for a little over half a mile through four gates before dipping gradually to a final one giving access to the road serving Dry Howe.

Make a right here until a walled track on your left is reached. Beyond a gate, turn left following the wall along the field edge. The path is maintained after another gate as a walled lane, at the end of which a right is made. Follow the connecting lane to its terminus, where a gate gives onto the open fell. Directly ahead, the slender cairn surmounting Whiteside Pike is clearly visible and easily attained along an exposed band of layered rock. It is possible with a little stretching of the hamstrings to complete the final 100 yards without setting boot on grass. Good luck! This eminent pinnacle deserves a higher status than previously accorded and is most assuredly the unsung hero in this remote backwater.

Follow a thin track through the heather, making a north-westerly course to a junction of walls where a stile is crossed. Bear left away from the ridge wall to climb Todd Fell, which is relegated to a subsidiary summit in view of its bald dome. If every visitor were to bring a stone to the top, perhaps in another 100 years its status could be re-appraised.

Make for the corner where the ridge wall heads west down into Long-sleddale. An unofficial stile can be negotiated to gain access to the right side of a continuing fence. Walking is made easier alongside a drainage ditch. Where it bends away right, keep to the ridge, passing through a cross-fence gate before rising gently up to Capplebarrow, the actual summit of which can only be gained by climbing the fence. Such unlawful activity cannot of course be condoned, can it?

Beyond another gate, a clear track points the way along the fence to the highest cairn on the horseshoe at Swinklebank. The substantial bonnet can be easily gained through a hole in the fence, after which we round the upper reaches of Bannisdale.

Where the fence heads off due north towards Sleddale Fell, swing away to the south east across the desolate bog of Borrowdale Moss. Join the ridge wall/fence for the return journey along the north side of the valley. Beyond the roughly-textured eminence of Long Crag, a wall gap is made awkward by a step-over fence, which places one's nether regions in some degree of jeopardy should the manoeuvre be miscalculated.

Continue along the wall, ascending the north flank of White Howe and veering due south once the gradient eases to reach the concrete trig column. From here, drop down into the depression and over the stileless fence, after which a broken wall allows free access to the nameless summit beyond.

After this, an increasingly steep descent must be made, but take care over the hidden crags of Capplefall. After landing safely at the bottom, follow the lines of old ditches to a gate in the cross wall. Keep right of the fence around the west side of Lamb Pasture, which close observation and a quick hand revealed had once (but not thankfully at the time of passing) been electrified.

At the next fence, pass through the gap on the left remembering to duck under the remaining top strand. A gate close to the concrete hut gives access to the far side of the fence. From here, head south swinging left away from the fence to follow a groove below the broken outcropping. The thin trail descends a grass slope joining a lower fell track at another fence. Take this track through the gate, keeping close to the wall on your right until another is reached. Accompany this one through a gate heading right down to a metalled lane.

Another right and a short stroll past a couple of cottages take you back to the parking place and the culmination of a trek into some of the remotest terrain within the National Park boundary — just!

22. THE HUB OF LAKELAND

Start and Finish: Cross the River Rothay at the farming hamlet of Ghyll Foot to park on the wide grass verge.

Summits Climbed:	Steel Fell	— 1811 feet
	Calf Crag	— 1762 feet
	High Raise	— 2500 feet
	Sergeant Man	— 2414 feet
	Tarn Crag	— 1801 feet

Total Height Climbed: 2800 feet

Distance Walked: 10 miles

Nearest Centre: Grasmere

Maps Required: Lying at the hub of the Lake District, all the Ordnance Survey English Lakes 1:25000 sheets are needed

INTRODUCTION

Much controversy has centred around the effects of low-flying aircraft in the Lake District but it appears that their presence is here to stay. Certainly, on this midweek expedition, they were buzzing the valleys like a swarm of killer bees. It is quite a strange feeling to look down on these denizens of the sky as one climbs up onto the elevated ridges.

Lying at what has come to be regarded as the 'centre' of Lakeland, and the hub of the wheel, this circuit of noble fells provides a supreme introduction to the core region. High Raise itself is reputed to be the pivot and is indeed the loftiest of the central fells with splendid all-round views.

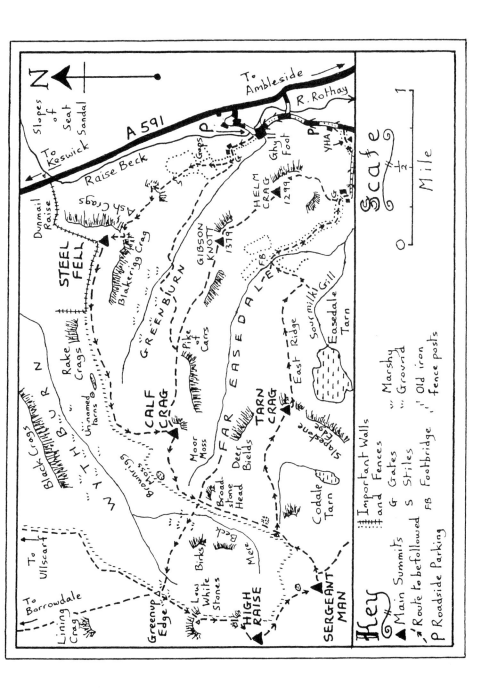

ROUTE DESCRIPTION

If you do not object to the mile of road walking at the termination of this walk, then park at Ghyll Foot and head north up the access track serving a pair of renovated cottages. Immediately beyond these, pass through a gate to enter the delightfully secluded Greenburn Valley. Turn right to follow the in-take wall through a series of gaps. These lower slopes are carpeted in bracken, which smothers the walls in summer.

A stile gives onto the open fell and a clear grass causeway points the way up the south ridge. This direct ascent surmounts a couple of crusty outcrops before the gradient eases on the rolling summit plateau and the pink cairn, sometimes referred to as Dead Pike, is reached.

Sited at a corner of what used to be the county boundary between Westmorland and Cumberland, we leave the summit and take the path beside a fence, which pursues a wide parabolic swing around the head of Greenburn. After the fence veers north down into Wythburn, a continuous line of iron fence posts indicates the way to Broadstone Head. In the depression, a family of tarns are passed on the right. Not mentioned on Ordnance Survey one inch maps prior to 1966, it is pleasing to see that they have now been included, although still un-named.

As the track begins to rise, bear left along a thin trod that diverts to the nobbly outlier of Calf Crag. From here, descend easy slopes to the head of Far Easedale, there to make a right crossing the marshy amphitheatre of Wythburn Head. Keep left under the shadowy configuration of Birks to stay dry-footed as progress is made up to the celebrated pass of Greenup Edge, the ancient packhorse route connecting Grasmere and Borrowdale.

Head left to follow a direct course south west, first over Low White Stones and thence due south to High Raise. Often referred to as High White Stones, the rash of bric-a-brac formed into a handy shelter provides welcome relief from the ever-present threat of strong westerlies. Sergeant Man can be seen below the grassy horizon a half-mile to the south east and is easily reached by following the accompanying fence posts.

Sergeant Man issues a bold challenge to those attacking from the south. Our approach exposes the chinks in his armour. The steep craggy descent to the east poses no problems. Cross the nameless beck feeding into Stickle Tarn to head east, keeping right of a substantial tarn close by. A thin trail joins with the old fence line again and begins to descend en route to Far Easedale Head.

Watch for a prominent rock tor after passing another smaller tarn. At this point, bear right to locate a stream-cut depression, which heads due east supplying the concealed Codale Tarn. The strengthening path is easy to follow and forks left away from the gully assuming a tortuous yet interesting route heading east towards Tarn Crag. This final summit overlooks the ever-popular Easedale Tarn but itself is rarely visited.

Once again, the abrupt downfall of the crag is only revealed when the neat summit cairn is reached. A direct descent to the east ridge is not recommended to land-fast mortals, who should make use of the gap separating the main top from the subsidiary summit. The splendid ridge provides an airy mile-long stroll on a good path, which eventually brings us to a T-junction.

Here take a left down into Far Easedale, crossing the footbridge and following the walled track down-valley. Beyond the wooded enclave of cottages, after passing through a gate, the way becomes metalled. Watch for the link route on your left, which enables a short cut to be made past a youth hostel, to reach the Ghyll Foot road and thence back to the car.

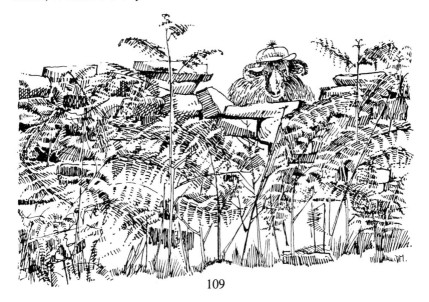

23. THE ESSENCE OF HERRIES COUNTRY

Start and Finish: A car park at the hamlet of Watendlath.

Summits Climbed:	High Tove	— 1665 feet
	Armboth Fell	— 1570 feet
	Ullscarf	— 2370 feet
	Great Crag	— 1500 feet
Total Height Climbed:	2100 feet	
Distance Walked:	9 miles	
Nearest Centre:	Watendlath	
Map Required:	Ordnance Survey English Lakes 1:25000 North West area sheet	

INTRODUCTION

Winter must be the most advantageous season to visit the old Norse hamlet of Watendlath, or perhaps during a rare drought of high summer. Once isolated from external influences, this classic Lakeland settlement at the 'end of the lake' was catapulted to fame through the celebrated 19th-century novels of Hugh Walpole. The atmosphere conjured up from four volumes of the *Herries Chronicles* can however best be appreciated when the hordes of summer pilgrims have departed.

Entry to this elongated narrow side valley is by means of a single-track highway that frequently becomes clogged with summer traffic; many vehicles make an initial stop at that most famous of packhorse bridges — Ashness. Yet even the burgeoning tourist market cannot suppress its romantic sense of

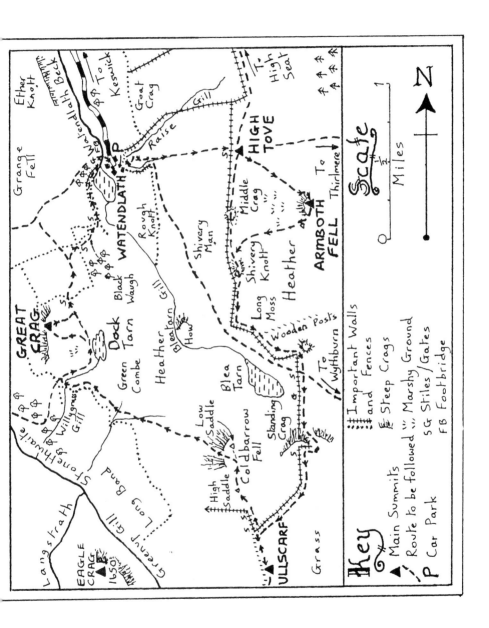

Key

🔺 Main Summits
Route to be followed
P Car Park

░░░ Important Walls and Fences
Steep Crags
Marshy Ground
SG Stiles/Gates
FB Footbridge

Scale

Miles

N

antiquity. Indeed, Walpole recognised the authentic character of this remote backwater when he described the landscape 'as a piece of gaily-tinted tapestry worked in English colours'.

When viewing the sharp outline of surrounding ice-crusted peaks honed to a razored image of perfection from the broad ridge, you may well indeed wonder what indefinable force has brought you here, when there is such a profusion of more celebrated fells within a five-mile radius. Yet the remote nature of this ridge is probably sufficient reason for your presence.

Unlike the upper fells in the vicinity, which are scored by numerous boundary fences, the enclosed in-bye pastures abutting Watendlath comprise traditional drystone walling described by Walpole as 'running like live things about the fells'. Just north of the hamlet, Watendlath Beck plunges over a chattering cataract known as the Devil's Punchbowl.

ROUTE DESCRIPTION

Cross the ladder stile on the north side of the car park and strike upstream on the right bank of Raise Gill. A gate allows access to the start of a zig-zag packhorse trail, which has unfortunately been subjected to the dubious attentions of the dreaded footpath rebuilders. Winding up the initial slope, bear left along a grooved way onto the open fell, where the gradient eases at 1250 feet and the final in-take wall shoots off due south in company with the Blea Tarn path.

Even in cold frosty conditions, the squelchy nature of the underlying turf is quite evident. Head east up the gently shelving plateau, passing through a fence stile to gain the summit of High Tove. The fence provides a comforting guide and link with reality when grey swirls of clinging mist shroud the heathery wilderness.

With little to keep us anchored hereabouts, the main track bound for Thirlmere is abandoned as we make a north-easterly bee-line across the depression, aiming for the distant Armboth Fell. When sunlight plays upon this broad expanse of open fell, it is hard to imagine that the tortured soul of a murdered Armboth bride is said to haunt the lonely sweep. Indeed, it is further claimed that all manner of unavenged spirits throughout the district gather upon the moor around the bewitching feast of Hallowe'en a phantom army to curdle the blood of the most sceptical bogtrotter.

Make a left-hand elliptical approach to the craggy oasis of Armboth Fell to avoid a boggy morass. Beyond the south cairn, recross the heather to join once again the ridge fence close to the outcropping known as Shivery Knott. Follow the old iron fence posts over the crest, continuing alongside the new creation, which makes a series of twists and turns before heading due south towards Standing Crag.

A direct assault is not to be encouraged, so bear left up a steepening grass slope to climb above the savage bastion and so rejoin the boundary fence. This can once again be followed along a clearly rising grass path until it veers sharply to the north. Stick with the old line of fence posts, which maintain a southerly course for a quarter-mile over the bald pate of Ullscarf and beyond. Lying as it does at the hub of the Lakeland dome is no doubt a sound enough reason why the Norse chieftain, Ulf, decided to immortalise his name atop this amorphous hump.

Returning northwards to the main fence, cross it via a stile to mount Coldbarrow Fell High Saddle. The clear path continues beyond towards Low Saddle but skirts left avoiding this outlier. Descend the bouldery slopes, aiming north west across the grassy plateau of Lord's How towards a wall corner.

Accompany the wall over hillocky terrain strewn with tough upland heather to meet the up-coming track from Stonethwaite. Bear right to follow Willygrass Gill in an easterly ascent to its source in Dock Tarn, beyond which a left fork is taken across the irregular confusion of low knolls. Maintain a general north-westerly course to gain Great Crag.

A clear yet narrow path heads north east to join the well-used track from Dock Tarn on its return to Watendlath. Inside the first in-take wall, a series of green-topped posts provides a diversion around the enclosed bog before the track eventually enters a rough-walled lane skirting the west bank of Watendlath Tarn. The ancient packhorse bridge, of which this is another splendid example, takes you back to the cluster of stone buildings and the culmination of the walk.

24. CHOICEST LOWESWATER

Start and Finish: Approaching the hamlet of Loweswater from the B5289, parking space is available adjacent to the telephone box at a Y-junction.

Summits Climbed:		
	Red Pike	— 2479 feet
	Starling Dodd	— 2085 feet
	Great Borne	— 2019 feet
	Gavel Fell	— 1720 feet

Total Height Climbed: Route A 3450 feet
Route B 1400 feet

Distance Walked: Route A 12 miles
Route B   8 miles

Nearest Centre: High Lorton

Map Required: Ordnance Survey English Lakes 1:25000, North West area sheet

INTRODUCTION

Here is a rare opportunity to accompany the author on a truly memorable hike into the fastness of western Lakeland, only to be attempted when clear weather can be guaranteed. If ever the time should arrive when I have the good fortune to be able to choose my place of retirement, then Loweswater must surely rank high on the selection list. Here is the perfect uncommercialised idyll where life drifts along at the sedate pace of an ambling tortoise.

To the south east, soaring monoliths jostle for a position of eminence on either flank of the Buttermere Valley. Is it little wonder that the legendary Wainwright requested that his ashes be scattered upon the crusty pate of his

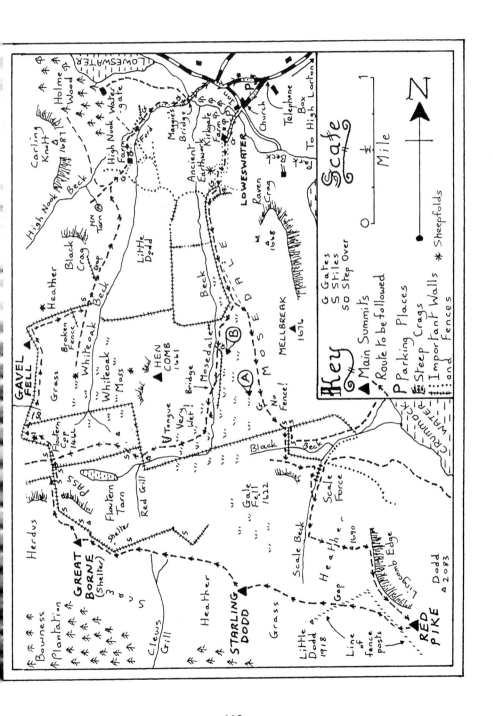

revered Haystacks? Nowhere else in Lakeland has the natural sculpture produced such a magnificent choice of routes to whet the appetite of the lone hiker.

Yet behind this imposing façade lies Mosedale. Hidden from prying eyes by the impressive Mellbreak, this valley lies no more than a mile from bustling Crummock yet displays all the attributes of a truly remote outpost. The name, originating from old Norse meaning 'valley of the bog', occurs frequently in Lakeland and all such dales are avoided by the majority of walkers because of their boggy nature. Double-wax your boots before setting out!

The main ridge system, which begins at High Crag, veers away from the Buttermere Valley to form the northern rampart of Ennerdale, the one valley in Lakeland that I have yet to set foot in. Viewed from above, the massed phalanx of conifers can be seen to hold sway over the lower slopes in uniform precision. Perhaps this is the appearance that much of the terrain exhibited in ancient times before the influx of Neolithic tribes led to an extensive forest clearance as farming communities sought to establish their tenuous hold on the virgin landscape.

ROUTE DESCRIPTION

From the telephone box parking area, carry on along the road to Loweswater hamlet, past the church and over the crossroads. Cross Park Beck, immediately after the Kirkstile Inn, heading up the narrow lane to Kirkgate Farm. An over-abundance of stone chippings makes your progress sound like the crunching of broken glass. Ahead, Mellbreak dominates the foreground.

Beyond the farm, the bridleway assumes a more characteristic appearance, rough underfoot and walled as far as a gate. Make a right here and follow the main track, with a small planting of conifers on your left. Head south up secluded Mosedale accompanying a strip steel fence, weathered a deep brown over many years.

When the fence forks right to cross the valley floor, a choice has to be made. Decisions, decisions. If your granny has been left propping up the bar in the Kirkstile Inn, perhaps you would be wiser to take the shorter 'B' route.

Should your ageing relative enjoy a penchant for the odd tipple (medicinal, of course), then bear right to follow the bridleway across to the far side of Mosedale. Having crossed the beck and right under the south flank of Hen Comb, be prepared for one of the wettest one thirds of a mile in Lakeland. A steady climb on grass heading west will bring you to Floutern, one of the least known of Lakeland passes.

Lone hikers, or those with tea-drinking grannies, will no doubt fork left to climb round the southern promontory of Mellbreak, passing a lone gate that has mislaid its fence. Upon reaching a wire fence, mount the right of two stiles and descend the grass bank to cross Black Beck. Join the path on the far side and follow it down to Scale Beck.

The path on the right of Scale Force (the highest cataract in Lakeland) avoids the crowds but unfortunately does not provide the best vantage point from which to view the waterfall. Above the falls, cross Scale Beck and follow a broad track through the heathery carpet to a prominent cairn on the skyline. This part of the climb requires a head-down approach, the pile of stones never seeming to get any closer!

Eventually arriving at Lingcomb Edge, a delightful path threads a merry course above the rim of crags towards the imposing cone of Red Pike. An expansive vista now unfolds along the full length of this high-level ridge, and across Ennerdale where Pillar Rock assumes a proud and solid bearing. Swing west away from the summit towards a line of fence posts, which can be accompanied back down the ridge, until a thin trail forks left to cross the rising swell of Little Dodd. Short springy turf makes this a fast passage, which is continued north west across the upland heather beyond Starling Dodd.

After the next depression, join with the fence and follow it up into the niche between the knotty twins of Great Borne. The main top, complete with trig column and shelter, lies on the left amid a welter of rocks, heather and bilberry couches — an ideal spot to linger on a late summer's afternoon before rejoining the path and fence for the steep descent of Steel Brow to Floutern Pass. Two fence stiles bring you to the main bridleway.

Go straight across up the pathless grass slope, sticking to the fence on your left. Just beyond a sheep pen, the fence turns sharp right. After 100 yards, a junction fence has to be crossed at a point where the upper strands of wire have been bent down by others who have passed this way with equal concern for the safety of their vitals. Beyond the depression occupied by an infant Grains Gill, pure grass gives way to some minor outcrops on White Oak, after which the fence leads you unerringly over the remarkable top of Gavel Fell, but just yards away from the true summit. Bear right and accompany it down the eastern flank into the valley of Whiteoak Beck.

When the main valley path is reached, cross a well-worn stile to head north. Pass through a fence gap after 100 yards, continuing down-valley and bearing left around the north-east shoulder to enter a side valley occupied by High Nook Tarn. Soon after the merging of two paths, go through a gate in the first in-take wall, following another down to High Nook Farm. Few strangers would seem to pass this way judging from the canine cacophony.

Through the farmyard, stick with the rough access road to cross Maggie's Bridge, after which it is upgraded to metalled lane. At the end and a T-junction, take a right and pursue a gentle course back to the car, hoping that granny hasn't eloped with the local shepherd.

25. THE OLD MAN CELEBRATES

Start and Finish: A lay-by at Haws Bank, south of Coniston at GR 299966, provides excellent parking on the left side of the A593.

Summits Climbed:	The Old Man of Coniston	— 2633 feet
	Brim Fell	— 2611 feet
Total Height Climbed:	2400 feet	
Distance Walked:	8 miles	
Nearest Centre:	Coniston	
Map Required:	Ordnance Survey English Lakes 1:25000, South West area sheet	

INTRODUCTION

The year 1993 marked the bicentennial celebrating the first tourist ascent of a mountain whose name is held in affectionate regard by the whole nation. Everybody, from pontiffs to politicians, girl guides to grandmothers and tramps to toffs, has made the pilgrimage up to the lofty pinnacle of Coniston Old Man. A one-armed soldier by the name of Captain Joe Budworth is credited with the first recorded conquest, one year after his embryonic climb of Helvellyn.

A locally-conceived meaning of Old Man stems from 'alt maen' (early miner), which is an appropriate name for a fell that is pockmarked with the ravages of the mining industry. Copper and slate are the chief sources of wealth that the Old man has bequeathed.

Coniston is the centre from which most ascents of the Old Man commence, a village that has managed to retain its dignity under an onslaught of tourism.

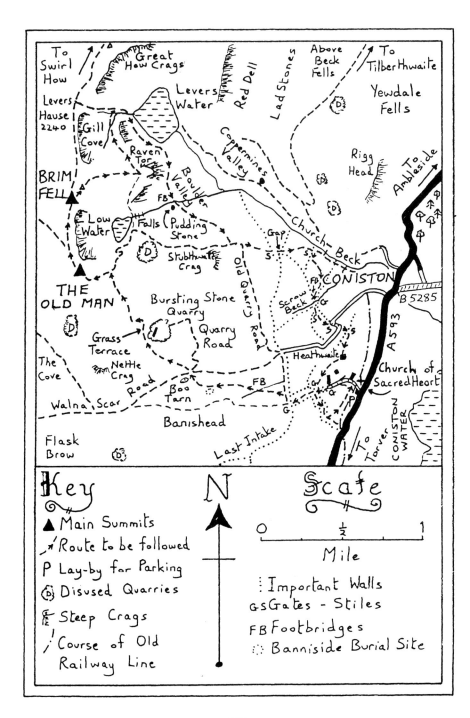

Key

▲ Main Summits
↗ Route to be followed
P Lay-by for Parking
(D) Disused Quarries
⚡ Steep Crags
⁞ Course of Old
    Railway Line

N

Scale

0   ½   1

Mile

⁞ Important Walls
G-S Gates - Stiles
FB Footbridges
⁛ Banniside Burial Site

Formerly an ancient Norse king's settlement, it prospered from the exploitation of copper mined in the valley of Levers Water to the north. The scars of this once-thriving industry are patently obvious on the lower slopes and it is only the upper fells that remain free of Man's scourging hand.

Approaching by way of Windermere from the east, the elongated ridge of the Coniston Fells gives no intimation of the Old Man's hidden stature. Only when observed from the south en route from Greenodd can the ageing dinosaur establish himself as an authentic and worthy guardian of the Coniston Valley.

ROUTE DESCRIPTION

From the road side lay-by abutting a wooden shelter, walk north for 50 yards before turning left up a lane past the Church of the Sacred Heart on your right. The metalled lane winds uphill under the old railway track to a row of four cottages. Continuing as a rough track, this initial section of the walk can be followed more easily on the large scape map overleaf.

After crossing the beck, make your way eastwards up to a gate in the last in-take wall. Bear right along the wall for 100 yards to the next field boundary, when the main path is abandoned in favour of a faint grooved path forking left across the open grass plateau. A wooded footbridge originally laid for the benefit of travellers has now been outgrown by the water course, which has isolated the structure in mid-stream. Continue in a westerly direction, aiming for the rising quarry road ahead.

Take note of the Banishead burial site, an ancient stone circle located at grid reference 285967, which was discovered in 1909. Bone ash and a child's teeth were unearthed after a cremation carried out during the Bronze Age, approximately 3000 years ago. Emerging close to the reedy pool known as Boo Tarn alongside Walna Scar Road, cross over and follow a grass track up the steepening slope of the Old Man's torso. This route is a delight to tread, being narrow and strategically cairned.

Climbing above Bursting Stone Quarry, a grass terrace heads north above the workings before swinging sharp left to make a tortuous ascent to meet the principal tourist route just below the summit. A left here quickly brings us

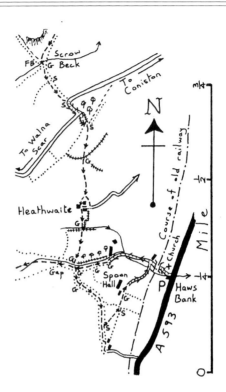

to the balding skull, capped by a slate dais complete with bobble hat. Overlooking the abrupt downfall towards Low Water, the lonely trig column stands aloof and neglected.

The half-mile north to Brim Fell is a simple stroll and provides a far more pleasing location for lunch. Thereafter, bear north east before veering east down a jutting shoulder to reach the Raven Tor col. Head left along a clear path into the upper reaches of Gill Cove, a secluded and remote dell that becomes pathless as height is lost.

Cross the beck to join the path descending from Levers Hause, which wends south east above Levers Water. Pass between a series of fenced mine shafts to climb over the lip into Boulder Valley. Pursue a leisurely descent among the scattering of large stones to traverse Low Water Beck, beyond which an enormous boulder has come to repose. The mammoth Pudding

Stone makes a perfect bench to marvel at the cascade of water diving off the rim of the back wall.

Continue along the miners' track to join the main route connecting the top quarry with Coniston. Make a left and almost immediately another, to depart from this over-burdened highway. Take the path that forks down parallel to Church Beck. Over the ladder stile, turn right beside the wall to meet an upper and infinitely less-trampled path.

Maintain a south-east bearing prior to swinging away right in company with a wall to cross Scrow Beck via a footbridge. From this point, make further use of the large-scale map, which details this latter section of our return to civilisation. After negotiating the metalled road serving the quarries, head south bound for Heathwaite. Pass between farm buildings in order to keep right of a field fence, and then across another field to emerge back onto the outward bridleway.

Cross straight over to follow a walled farm lane, which funnels down into a rough tree-lined conduit. Take the wooden stile on your left, which indicates a newly-created alternative route. Aim north east for a white-painted narrow slab stile to pass close to Spoon Hall. A short stroll down the access road leads back to the main highway.

26. HELVELLYN — AT LAST!

Start and Finish: A lakeside car park located 200 yards south of Glenridding Bridge.

Summits Climbed:	Birkhouse Moor	— 2334 feet
	Helvellyn	— 3118 feet
	White Side	— 2832 feet
	Raise	— 2889 feet

Total Height Climbed: 3250 feet

Distance Walked: 10 miles

Nearest Centre: Glenridding

Map Required: Ordnance Survey English Lakes 1:25000, North East area sheet

INTRODUCTION

In contrast to those other major summits in Wales and the Isle of Man, which are a mere train ride away from conquest, Helvellyn has thus far managed to shake off any attempts at modernisation. It is without doubt one of the most popular mountains in the country. From Land's End to John O' Groats, the mention of its name raises eyebrows of recognition more than any other and it remains a giant far beyond the confines of hiking clubs. The ascent described here includes the unchallenged classic route between the Hole-in-the-Wall and Helvellyn summit, and as such tends to suffer from over-population in high season. Nonetheless, the thrill and excitement of balancing gingerly along the serrated rib of Striding Edge always quickens the heartbeat no matter how often one returns.

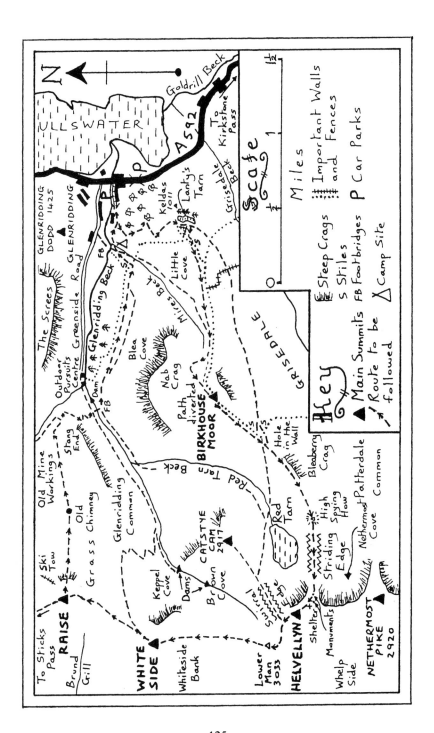

Scale

Miles

| 0 | ½ | 1 | 1½ |

Key

🔺 Main Summits

➴ Route to be followed

⧦ Steep Crags

S Stiles

FB Footbridges

P Car Parks

⛺ Camp Site

⣿ Important Walls and Fences

N

ULLSWATER

Goldrill Beck

A 592

To Kirkstone Pass

P

Griisedale Beck

Keldas 1011

Lantys Tarn

GLENRIDDING DODD 1425

GLENRIDDING

The Screes

Outdoor Pursuits Centre

Greenside Road

Glenridding Beck

Dam

FB

FB

Mires Beck

Little Cove

Blea Cove

Nab Crag

Path diverted

GRISEDALE

BIRKHOUSE MOOR

Hole in the Wall

Bleaberry Crag

Old Mine Workings

Stang End

Ski Tow

Old Grass Chimney

Glenridding Common

Red Tarn Beck

Red Tarn

High Spying How

Nethermost Cove

Patterdale Common

To Sticks Pass

Brund Grill

RAISE

WHITE SIDE

Whiteside Bank

Keppel Cove

Dams

Brown Cove

CATSTYE CAM 2917

Swirral Edge

Striding Edge

Lower Man 3033

HELVELLYN

Shelter

Monuments

Whelp Side

NETHERMOST PIKE 2920

Helvellyn was first climbed out of pure curiosity in 1792 by that veteran defender of the realm, one-armed Captain Joe Budworth, who delighted in rolling boulders off the summit into Red Tarn below — not a pursuit likely to endear him to the present day followers of the country code, nor those struggling manfully up the final east tower.

And so it is that people return time after time to tread a wide variety of routes up to the hallowed summit. But be prepared; even Helvellyn addicts can come to grief in low mist or wintery conditions if they fail to appreciate the potential dangers. An eminent cragsman, one John Dalton, once found himself enveloped in the densest cloud on the summit plateau. Clutching grimly to each other's coats, he and his companions proceeded onward in what was thought to be the correct direction when suddenly the old man froze, his boot raised to continue, before gasping out, 'Not a step more. There is nothing but cloud to tread on.' A propitious break in the clouds had revealed they were perched on the brink of the precipice overlooking Red Tarn — a near thing, and one we should all take heed of.

ROUTE DESCRIPTION

From the lakeside car park, return to Glenridding Bridge and take a left down the side road, which soon becomes a stony track. From here, make use of the large-scale map opposite for your climb up the wooded valley flank. On an ascent of the north-facing slope, in early spring, one cannot fail to be moved by the vivid azure of bluebells en route to Lanty's Tarn.

On this particular walk, drought had left the tarn in a somewhat reduced state. At mid-point, head right alongside the small fenced conifer plantation to meet the ridge wall, which is crossed via a stile after 100 yards. A thin path strengthens as height is gained. Stick close to the right side of the wall as it snakes up and over the top of Birkhouse Moor. Prior to the final assault, a diversionary zig-zag allows the badly-eroded section time for rejuvenation.

There is little need to pause on the featureless plateau, so continue along the wall until it veers abruptly south east at the gap known familiarly to hikers as the 'Hole-in-the-Wall' (now blocked by a fence stile). The clear route ahead climbs gradually around the prominent rock tower, which guards the

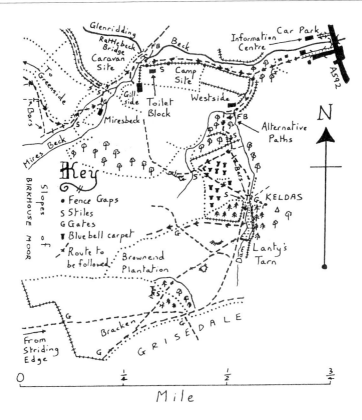

Key

- Fence Gaps
- S Stiles
- G Gates
- Bluebell carpet
- Route to be followed

beginning of Striding Edge. The Edge falls away steeply to adjacent corries on either side. For the best sport, stick to the sharp rim, although less adventurous persons are catered for below the lip.

There follows a steep assault on the shattered ramparts above Red Tarn, which leads directly to the memorial dedicated to a faithful hound who stayed beside his master for three months in 1803 following the latter's untimely demise — a clear indication of how often the mountain was climbed in those days. Another plaque commemorating the landing of an aircraft on the summit plateau in 1926 is located close to the cross-wall shelter. The summit proper lies just to the north, teetering on the brink of a sharp drop.

To avoid the inevitable throng, lunch is best taken atop the subsidiary peak of Lower Man, overlooking the remote corrie of Brown Cove. A stony descent to the north is followed by a brief saunter up the facing bank on to White Side, after which a further shallow depression is crossed. Leave the main path here, which pursues a tortuous course down into Keppel Cove, and aim up the next slope. A grassy level terminates our roller coasting along the ridge, after which the gnarled summit of Raise is gained; the top is a confused array of weathered boulders, in contrast to the generally smooth appearance of the local fells.

The ridge track becomes increasingly less distinct as it continues north down to Sticks Pass. Once a well-used pack horse trail for the region's natural resources, particularly lead from the Greenside Mine, it is now the sole preserve of the modern fell trekker. Our way lies due east, however, down a long grassy flank, the monotony of which is broken by an isolated rash of shattered rock fragments below an outcropping. Watch out for the ski lift, which the gentle slopes encourage in the event of a white winter. Further down, the slope is compressed between Sticks Gill and Rowten Beck into a narrow arm beyond the ruined chimney. A clear path follows the old aqueduct down to meet the miners' track continuing down to Greenside. Turn right along the zig-zag trail, through junipers, below the towering elbow of Stang End. The Outdoor Pursuits Centre is clearly visible.

Upon gaining the valley route, cross the footbridge immediately upstream from a weir to join a splendid path above the in-take wall. Head left down-valley, keeping with the quieter lower section, until a stile is reached immediately prior to Mires Beck. Bear left down to the valley floor, then right alongside the large camp site to rejoin the outward route back to Glenridding.

My son Steve accompanied me on this walk and managed the circuit with flying colours. He was soon pressing hard for the 'big boy'; the Roof of England was completed before the year was out using the route described at the end of this book.

27. BEHIND THE GRAND FACADE

Start and Finish: Continuing north beyond the hamlet of Mosedale, take the road for Hesket Newmarket for a quarter-mile until
the accompanying wall veers away to the right. Ample parking
space is available on the open grass verge.

Summits Climbed:	Carrock Fell	— 2174 feet
	Knott	— 2329 feet
	Great Calva	— 2265 feet

Total Height Climbed: 2550 feet

Distance Walked: 13 miles

Nearest Centre: Mungrisdale

Map Required: Ordnance Survey Landranger
Series 90 1:50000, Penrith, Keswick
and Ambleside sheet

INTRODUCTION

Approaching from the direction of Grasmere, the northern panorama of
Lakeland is dominated by Skiddaw and Blencathra, extrovert giants who
display their best attributes in the front window. For most visitors, their
imposing might is a challenge impossible to resist.

Few people bother to get acquainted with the rolling grass-clad fells that
are hidden from casual view behind the glossy façade and locally referred to as
the fells at the 'back o' Skidda'. Yet here you can wander at will, unhindered
by walls or fences, in splendid isolation. Even on a bank holiday, you are
guaranteed a degree of seclusion that few of the more eminent summits could
ever offer. When traversing the ridge between Carrock Fell and Knott, take

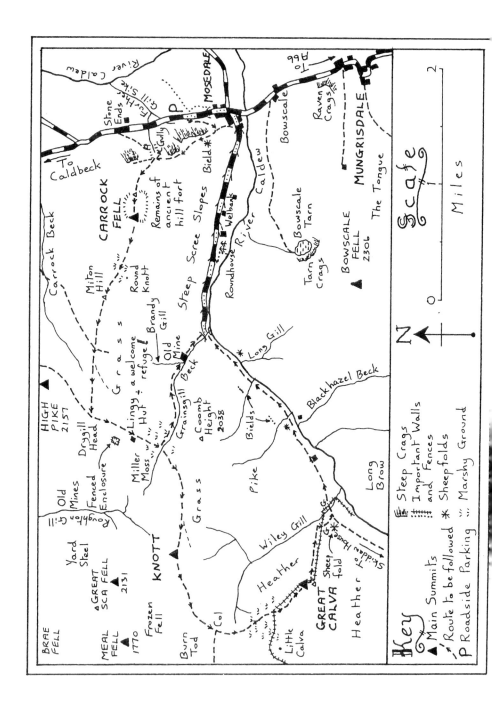

time out for a brief sojourn at the hut on Great Lingy Hill. Once a shooting hut, but now maintained by the National Park Management Services, it provides welcome shelter from the elements for cross-country travellers. The diary inside makes for interesting reading whilst tarrying for lunch.

According to a notice pinned up inside, over 1000 visitors make use of Lingy Hut every year. Averaging out at something like three a day, you are an odds-on favourite to have it to yourself. On a previous visit, the diary had gone walkabout and I was unable therefore to fill it in; perhaps it has gone to join its ancestors at the final resting place in the Blencathra Field Centre.

ROUTE DESCRIPTION

Cross the road at the wall corner and follow a faint track that climbs obliquely back above Mosedale. This rough and steeply sloping south east rampart of Carrock Fell presents no difficulty as the path picks a gradual course up through the rock garden. As it swings round into the Caldew Valley, watch out for the main track coming up from below. Join it and head right up the scree-choked south-east shoulder.

Continue beyond a wall bield across the easy yet pathless heathery slopes, making your way in a gradual rise towards the abrupt dry gully occupied by the lower reaches of Further Gill Syke. Climb above the gully on a clear trail that follows the edge of the crags. But watch for a left fork, which mounts the upper slope to gain the elongated hill fort summit of Carrock Fell.

This is the only Iron Age hill fort in the Lake District. It dates from around 80 AD and was constructed by the Brigantes, an ancient Celtic tribe eventually quelled by the invading Roman legions, who destroyed much of the fortification. Nevertheless, the extent of the surrounding citadel is clearly visible and remains one of my favourite spots for quiet meditation. Sit awhile and ponder the violent activity that must have taken place in days gone by in contrast to the peace that now emanates from this special place.

Head west along the broad ridge on a fair path that skirts Round Knott and aims for the distinctive cairn on Miton Hill. Across a shallow depression, the path ascends the facing grass bank over Drygill Head to meet the principal right of way at the top of the Caldbeck Fells. Bear left down to the unique edifice of Lingy Hut. Don't forget to keep the hut clean and fasten the door when you leave.

The continuing path disappears in the swampy morass of Miller Moss. Keep to a south-westerly course, and the path can soon be seen climbing the steepening bank ahead. A choice now has to be made. The shorter way lies down Grainsgill Beck. Take a left at the depression to accompany the right bank of the narrow V-shaped valley along a thin trail that soon forms in the tussocky heather. This crosses to the far side upstream from the beck's junction with Brandy Gill as the abandoned ruins of Carrock Mine are approached.

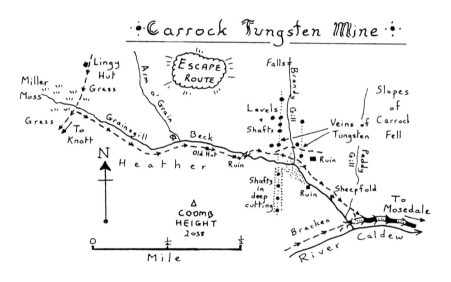

Once the only source of tungsten (wolfram) in Lakeland, the open shafts are a hypnotic attraction to young hikers, who should be strongly curtailed from pursuing their natural curiosity to explore. Useful because of its hardening and high melting properties, dead straight veins can be seen at right angles to Grainsgill Beck on either side of Brandy Gill. Old mines abound in the National Park (see map accompanying Walk 16), all of which can be a threat to continued enjoyment of the fells if due care is not taken.

132

A half-mile beyond the mine workings, the wide track merges at a point where the tarmacked access road up the Caldew Valley ends. A leisurely stroll down to Mosedale completes a shorter though no less highly interesting alternative.

Tough guys and those of independent spirit should mount the grass slope west of Comb Height before continuing west along the blunt ankle-jarring shoulder of Knott. A gentle ascent on a thin path takes you up onto this commanding height.

In order to attain our final objective, Great Calva, a wide sweep around the cutting of Wiley Gill must be made by first descending a grass slope to the col above Hause Gill. Mounting the opposite side, the path swings south east across an unpleasant area of marsh until an old iron fence is reached. Follow this onto the splendid cone of Great Calva, which is undoubtedly one of the pre-eminent summits in the northern fells.

The mountain forms the northern extremity of a huge rift that cleaves the district in two. This elongated trough provides an essential north-south communications link, as well as an unexpectedly far-reaching viewpoint. From the immediate foreground of the Glenderaterra Valley south, through St. John's-in-the-Vale, to Thirlmere and the Vale of Grasmere, you gain the impression of being able to observe South Lakeland through a mountain tunnel.

Immediately before the south top, head due west alongside a fence down the steep yet direct descent towards Wiley Gill. As the stream is approached, pass through a gate and join the valley track serving Skiddaw House. Bear left to ford Wiley Gill and through a gate to accompany the River Caldew down to the Carrock Mine access road. Here the road becomes metalled but still makes a pleasant if rather protracted return to Mosedale. Make a left through the huddle of cottages to meet the lower road, which will return you to your car.

28. BUTTERMERE'S PRESTIGIOUS WATERSHED

Start and Finish: Pull off the road a half-mile east of Gatesgarth on the left of the B5289.

Summits Climbed:

Fleetwith Pike	—	2126 feet
Grey Knotts	—	2287 feet
Brandreth	—	2344 feet
Haystacks	—	1940 feet

Total Height Climbed: 2800 feet

Distance Walked: 7½ miles

Nearest Centre: Buttermere/Seatoller

Map Required: Ordnance Survey English Lakes 1:25000, North West area sheet

INTRODUCTION

It is often the case that the Lake District can be split across the middle, north and south experiencing vastly differing conditions. On one of my recent visits to the southern fells, I found them swathed in a grey mist and was almost tempted to give up and call it a day. However, a niggling reluctance to succumb, plus eternal optimism, that essential ingredient found in every fell wanderer's rucksack, led me on a tortuous course over into Buttermere. My faith was rewarded with clear views and a cloud base hovering around 2700 feet.

The Buttermere Valley, a classic of its type in glacial terms, is best admired in all its splendour from the knife-edged spine of Fleetwith Pike. Like the

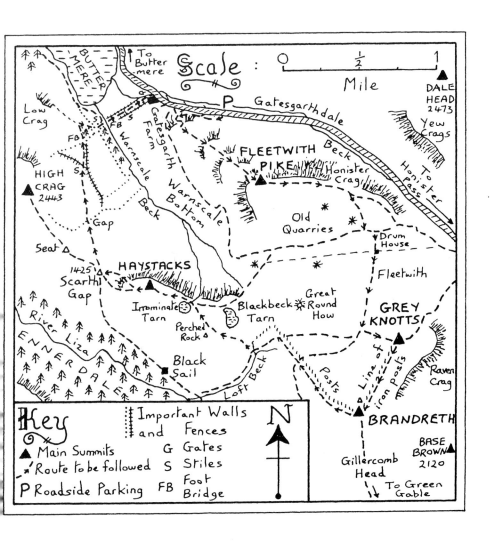

Scale:

0   ½   1

Mile

BUTTERMERE

To Buttermere

P   Gatesgarthdale

DALE HEAD 2473

Yew Crags

Low Crag

FB

S

Gatesgarth Farm

FLEETWITH PIKE

Honister Crag

To Honister Pass

HIGH CRAG 2443

Ford

S

Warnscale Beck

Warnscale Bottom

Old Quarries

Gap

Drum House

Seat △

Fleetwith

1425 △

HAYSTACKS

Scarth Gap

Innominate Tarn

Blackbeck Tarn

Great Round How

GREY KNOTTS

River Liza

ENNERDALE

Perched Rock △

Black Sail

Loft Beck

Posts

Line of iron Posts

Raven Crag

BRANDRETH

Key

⋮ Important Walls and Fences

G   Gates

S   Stiles

FB   Foot Bridge

N

▲ Main Summits

⤴ Route to be followed

P Roadside Parking

Gillercomb Head

To Green Gable

BASE BROWN 2120

prow of an ancient galley, the soaring ridge cleaves the valley head, splitting it in two and coming to anchor just short of the finger lake. Mere words fail to convey the aggressive grandeur of this most prestigious of valleys. So get those boots on and sample its delights at first hand — or foot.

ROUTE DESCRIPTION

From the pull-in, head back west towards Gatesgarth on a faint path rising gradually across the lower grass flanks of Fleetwith Pike. Join with the main track to make a left climbing the zig-zags up the slopes of Low Raven Crag. Much improved to a high standard of refurbishment, the initial steepness eases above the crag to pursue a direct course up the saw-toothed blade of Fleetwith Edge.

Mounting a series of rocky steps, the summit remains hidden from view until the final tower is breached. A continuously steep pull, the ascent poses no difficulties and leads to a splendid perch controlling the awesome prospect down-valley beyond Crummock Water.

Cross the top of High Crag and continue ahead on a good path along the gently-shelving ridge above the abrupt downfall of Honister Crag. Watch for an indistinct right fork, which carries you down through abandoned mine workings to cross the old slate tramway and link with the smuggler's trail known as Moses' Trod.

Head south for a half-mile until the Trod swings to the right. Leave it here to climb left heading in an easterly direction. The pathless grass leads to the rather obscure summit of Grey Knotts, a confused plateau of weathered outcroppings, each one vying for the privilege of being named principal cairn. If approaching from the east, the shape of the fell is more obvious and less of an enigma. Thereafter, follow a line of iron fence posts, which lead unerringly to the barren summit of Brandreth to the south south west.

From here, turn west to accompany the posts down over an ocean of stones aiming towards Buttermere. The lake winks serenely at you in the afternoon sun if you are thus favoured. Closer, the twin jewels of Black Beck and Innominate Tarns sparkle in the crowning glory that is Haystacks. Revered and honoured by many as being the pièce de résistance on the Buttermere round, it has become a hallowed place for devotees of the late AW whose ashes are scattered there. As a result, many of the paths have been turned into ugly highways by hordes of avid pilgrims.

Our route bears sharp left, prior to reaching the elevated upthrust of Great Round How, and then drops down to the upper reaches of Loft Beck ravine. Cross the beck to head north west along a thin trail that meanders amidst heather and bilberry. The track then merges with the main highway east of Innominate Tarn. A distinctive perched boulder is passed on your left. The rough ascent onto the summit ridge of Haystacks is soon accomplished, and a veritable feast of rampant crag scenery must be carefully negotiated.

The descent to Scarth Top is best undertaken along the less-frequented northern route, which is gained by keeping to the Buttermere side of the fell. Steep rock walls abound and hands a-plenty are needed to ease your passage down to the pass.

This grassy 'notch in the ridge', once an important pony route linking Wasdale and Buttermere, still provides a nostalgic through route for fell wanderers. The rocky hillocks of a somewhat similar contour in the region of Scarf Gap have become well-known in misty conditions for what is known as 'circular walking'. The story is told about a party of Victorian ladies journeying from Wasdale Head to Buttermere who were caught in the open hereabouts. One of them lost a pocket book and recovered it two hours later, proving that they had indeed been walking in a circle. When the mist finally lifted just before sunset, they were lucky enough to find themselves close to the path they had been seeking and so descended safely to Gatesgarth.

At the pass, bear right and follow a straightforward descent on a well-graded track to valley level. After crossing Warnscale Beck, a fence corridor allows for no deviation across the lush pasture land of the flat valley floor. Once the main road is gained, abutting Gatesgarth Farm, continue east towards Honister Pass for a half-mile, which returns us to the car pull-in.

29. HOGGET HIGHLIGHTS

Start and Finish: Pull in to a roadside parking area located 100 yards north of the Brotherswater Inn on the left of the A592.

Summits Climbed:		
	Little Hart Crag	— 2091 feet
	Red Screes	— 2541 feet
	Middle Dodd	— 2106 feet

Total Height Climbed: 2700 feet

Distance Walked: 7½ miles

Nearest Centre: Patterdale

Maps Required: Ordnance Survey English Lakes 1:25000, South East and North East area sheets

INTRODUCTION

Hidden within the left-hand arm of the short yet deeply-scoured Dovedale trough, Hogget Gill offers a gully scramble of the highest order. Few people tread the rock-strewn bed of the gill, assuring you a degree of remoteness and seclusion unprecedented in a locale so close to a major highway. A world apart, pathless and lonely, it remains free from intrusion by unseemly crowds that clog up the main arteries above.

The highpoint of this walk culminates atop the guardian of Kirkstone Pass. Red Screes has the unmistakeable appearance of an upturned rowing boat when approached from the south west. This was my first Lakeland conquest undertaken with the local youth club in snow and ice thick enough to encourage sliding across the frozen summit tarn, a unique feature that no other Lake District fell can lay claim to. The original name of Kilnshaw

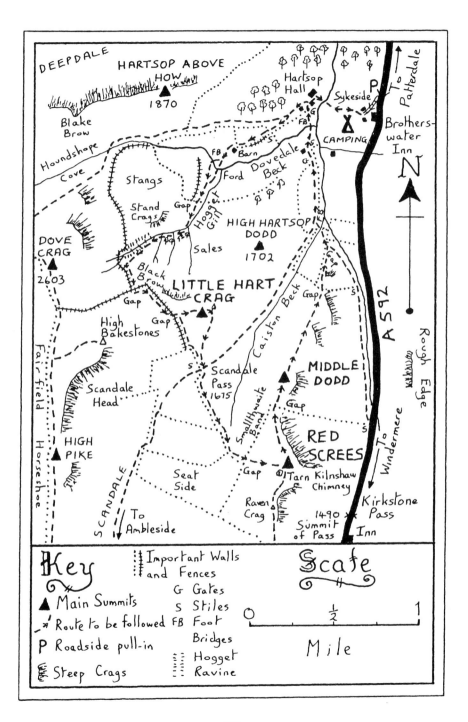

DEEPDALE

HARTSOP ABOVE

HOW
1870

Blake
Brow

Houndshope
Cove

Stangs

Stand
Crags

DOVE
CRAG
2603

Sales

Hogget Gill

Gap

Black
Brow

LITTLE HART
CRAG

Gap

Gap

High
Bakestones

Fairfield Horseshoe

Scandale
Head

HIGH
PIKE

SCANDALE

Seat
Side

To
Ambleside

Hartsop
Hall

Sykeside

CAMPING

Barn

Ford

FB

Dovedale
Beck

HIGH HARTSOP
DODD
1702

Caiston Beck

Gap

Scandale
Pass
1675

Smallthwaite Barn

Gap

MIDDLE
DODD

Gap

RED
SCREES

Tarn

Kilnshaw
Chimney

Raven
Crag

Gap

1490
Summit
of Pass

A 592

To Patterdale

P

N

Brothers-
water
Inn

Rough Edge

To
Windermere

Kirkstone
Pass

Inn

Key

Important Walls
and Fences

G Gates

S Stiles

FB Foot
Bridges

Hogget
Ravine

▲ Main Summits

Route to be followed

P Roadside pull-in

Steep Crags

Scale

0   ½   1

Mile

139

Chimney refers to the scree gully under the eastern rim overlooking the Kirkstone Pass Inn 800 feet below.

It has to be admitted, however, that one of my main motivations when planning this route was to include the north shoulder of Middle Dodd. After crossing this wedge-shaped prow, I was able to tick off my last mountain in the eastern fell region. Peak bagging is a sport most frequently indulged in by newcomers to fell walking, where the main aim is to amass a veritable hoard of conquests in the shortest possible time. Even after 20-plus years of fell wandering, I still have numerous outliers to notch up, particularly in the less accessible west of Lakeland.

ROUTE DESCRIPTION

Walk back up the A592 and fork right down the access road leading into Sykeside campsite. A track heads west, crossing Kirkstone Beck to gain the far side of the main valley and Hartsop Hall. This working farm has ingeniously adapted to the tourist market by encouraging guests to get involved in the day-to-day business of hill farming.

Enter the side valley of Dovedale along the lower path, which follows a wall south west as far as a stout barn. Thereafter, keep above Dovedale Beck, ignoring a ford to cross by means of a footbridge upstream. From here, head south into the unspoilt depths of this secluded dalehead. A thin trail passes through a wall gap to join with Hogget Gill, before making a sharp right into the lower wooded ravine.

The brooding overhang of Black Brow presents a solid defence of castellated battlements that rear up to dissuade all but the hardiest pioneer from venturing further. Hogget Gill provides excellent scrambling suitable for the adventurous fell wanderer who enjoys the close proximity of bare rock. Above the boulder-choked gorge, tumbling cataracts squeeze between crag spouts that need to be negotiated on the left. The steep banks are stepped and so enable the upper slopes to be ascended safely.

When the precipitous sides of the higher ravine prevent further progress in the bed of the gill, cut up the grass slope on the left to emerge onto gradually rising terrain where a fence crosses the watercourse. Bear left and follow the fence to where it joins with another in a T-junction. Cross this second fence and turn left to follow it around the undulating plateau above Black Brow.

Leave the main path where the fence bends south for Scandale Pass, crossing a broken section and heading due east to mount Little Hart Crag, a gnarled elbow that stands proud from the bleak grassy surroundings. Few people bother making a detour to visit this crusty outlier, which leaves the dual summit remote from unnecessary intrusion.

Upon departing, make an initial swing to the east and descend through the scattered rock debris onto easier ground. Make for the wall, which drops down to Scandale Pass. Beyond, the way leads up the facing slope in a direct path. Keep to the left side of the wall until its terminus. A gap in the cross-wall is followed by a short easterly stroll to the top of Red Screes. On a hot summer's day, take time out to bathe your feet in the summit tarn before heading north along the gently-shelving ridge bound for Middle Dodd.

Once you have crossed the broken ridge wall on Smallthwaite Band, there follows a brief grassy amble onto the narrow summit surrounded by a strange array of scooped ditches. The magnificent panorama north towards Ullswater is maintained on the direct descent to valley level. Continue down the sharp north ridge on a thin trod, which becomes increasingly steep as height is lost. Half-way down, a cross-wall is encountered and must be crossed, accompanying a north-bound wall downwards on its right. Keep tight to this wall if a close encounter with the Grim Reaper through premature crag flying is to be avoided.

Join with the Kirkstone path to head left, crossing Caiston Beck on a footbridge. Fork into the main path from Scandale Pass and continue north past a barn adjacent to an ancient Stone Age settlement. Another footbridge takes you back to Hartsop Hall. Thereafter, retrace your steps through the campsite.

141

30. CONTRASTS IN KENTMERE

Start and Finish: Roadside parking is available close to the church in Kentmere village. Take note that no cars are permitted beyond this point.

Summits Climbed:	Yoke	— 2309 feet
	Sallows	— 1691 feet
Total Height Climbed:	2100 feet	
Distance Walked:	8 miles	
Nearest Centre:	Kentmere	
Map Required:	Ordnance Survey English Lakes 1:25000, South East area sheet	

INTRODUCTION

Being one of the most southerly Lakeland valleys has made Kentmere a favoured destination when time is of the essence for those of us residing in this locale. Visitors who make the detour from the A591 will be amply rewarded.

An abrupt change in the nature of the underlying rock strata is manifestly evident on this walk, the Garburn Road marking a distinct separation between the ice-hewn splendour characteristic of the Borrowdale Volcanics to the north and a softer more undulating system observed in Silurian Slate topography. On no other walk could you possibly encounter such starkly differing elements in the geological framework. And the roadside parking at Kentmere Church lies directly across the line of this rift.

Once the lower valley slopes of woodland are left behind, the contrasting forces of nature that split Kentmere asunder can be readily appreciated.

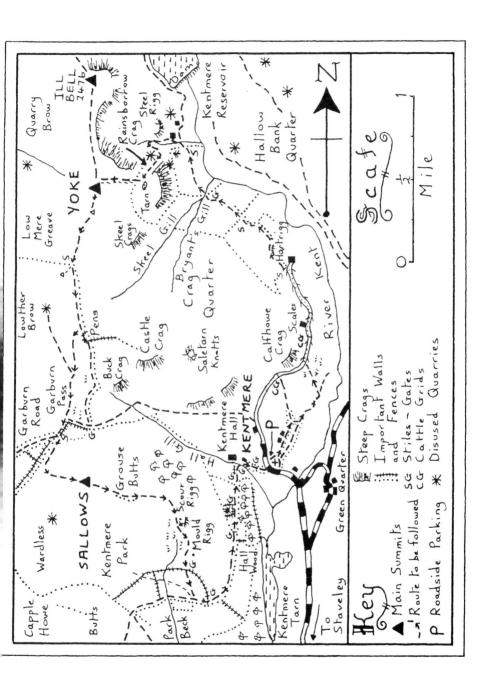

Key

ᗡ Main Summits

➜ Route to be followed

P Roadside Parking

▦ Steep Crags

⫶⫶⫶ Important Walls and Fences

SG Stiles ~ Gates

CG Cattle Grids

✳ Disused Quarries

Scale

0 ¼ ½ ¾ 1
Mile

N

Capple Howe

Butts

Wardless ✳

SALLOWS

Kentmere Park

Grouse Butts

Scour Rigg

Mould Rigg

Park Beck

Kentmere Tarn

Hall Wood.

To Staveley

Green Quarter

KENTMERE

Kentmere Hall

Garburn Road

Garburn Pass

Lowther Brow ✳

Buck Crag

Pens

Castle Crag

Saltarn Knotts

Calfhowe Crag

Scales

Low Mere Greave

YOKE

Skeel Crags

Skeel Gill

Bryant's Gill

Crag Quarter

Saltarn Quarter

Hartrigg

River Kent

Quarry Brow ✳

ILL BELL 2476

Rainsborrow Crag

Steel Rigg

Tarn

Kentmere Reservoir ✳

✳

Hallow Bank Quarter

143

Human conflict is also much in evidence as demonstrated at Kentmere Hall where a perfect example of a 14th-century pele tower has been incorporated into the farm proper.

Square with three storeys and a flat roof, the pele tower gave protection from marauding hordes of Scottish invaders. During its construction, the Troutbeck giant, Hugh Hird by name, is reputed to have single-handedly raised the 30-foot chimney beam into place, a Herculean task that had already defeated the efforts of ten men. Hugh eventually died from internal injuries sustained whilst engaged in his favourite pastime of ripping trees up by their roots.

The map below indicates the location of all pele towers around Lakeland and shows that most were built in the more vulnerable areas to the north. Only that in Kentmere lies in a remote valley location, which would appear to emphasise the cautious nature of the indigenous population at that time.

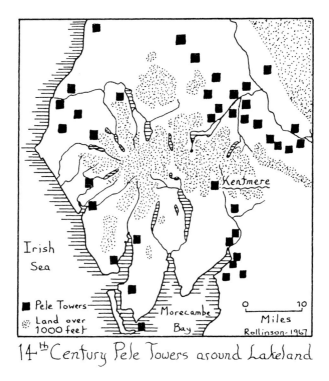

14ᵗʰ Century Pele Towers around Lakeland

144

ROUTE DESCRIPTION

Immediately to the left of the church, a track composed of loose chippings should be taken until a wall gate is reached on the right. Join the rough-walled lane beyond, which rises gradually before dipping to valley level. This initial section as far as the access road to Hartrigg can be followed using the large-scale map accompaniment.

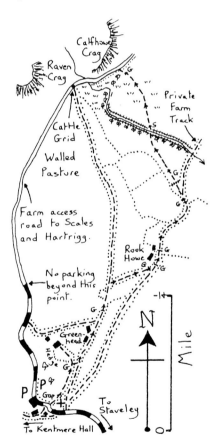

Turn left onto the metalled highway skirting the base of Calfhowe Crag. At Hartrigg, continue along the track, passing a small copse. Swing down left to the valley bottom. (Should you encounter Farmer Dawson, 40 years manager of all the pasture and rough fell on this side of the River Kent, take time out to make his acquaintance — an amiable and chatty agrarian indeed.) The path continues along to the renovated quarry buildings, with the savage bastion of Rainsborrow Crag overshadowing all. Note the small fenced enclosures en route where tiny conifers are being weaned. Are attempts being made to establish a plantation here? Let us hope not.

Behind the first building, slant left up the bracken-clad slope, hemmed in by buttressing grey rock on either side. Stick to the right side of the beck past a small group of conifers.

Upon entering the confines of Rainsborrow Cove, the gradient eases. Swing left up to the scattered remnants of an old slate quarry, taking note of a narrow ledge that slants up across the back wall from right to left. This thin trod crosses a decaying wall and provides access to the serrated north ridge of Rainsborrow Crag. Its ascent is heady stuff and requires a steady nerve and both hands. Avoid bearing too far south where scrambling assumes severe proportions beyond the capabilities of mere fell walkers. Those of a nervous disposition should keep both eyes focussed ahead.

Arriving at the climax of the toothy edge, crag gives way to tussocky grass. Keep right of a small tarn to follow a broken wall up to a line of fence posts arrowing due west. Now much decimated by the ravages of Lakeland's harsh climate, they do provide an unwavering pointer to Yoke's summit cairn.

The top of the mountain has little in common with its eastern flank and gives the mistaken impression of being a shapeless hump when approached along the main ridge. Head south along the broad plateau, which slants gradually down to a wall crossed by means of a stile. Keep on the right side of the wall until a fenced sheep pen is seen ahead. Fifty yards before this, fork right away from the wall, following a clear grass path that soon merges with an old quarry track. Maintain a south-bound course to reach the top of Garburn Pass — a once vital link between Troutbeck and the eastern valleys.

Join the Garburn Road until the fence terminates and the road becomes walled on its descent of the Troutbeck flank. Cross a stile on your left at this point and follow the continuing wall south west up an easy grass slope. Bear left at the crest across a grass moor onto the domed summit of Sallows. The narrow shale wedge marking the top maintains a cairn of diminutive proportions (three stones only at the last count). Visitors are asked to assist its growth.

Continue down the long sweeping south-east ridge past a line of defunct grouse shooting butts. The broad hummocky nature of the terrain appears somewhat confusing but is easily negotiated by keeping left and aiming for the table-topped summit of Scour Rigg. Follow a thin path on the right of this, which skirts the marshy source of Park Beck below Mould Rigg. After passing through a gated fence, aim for the bridleway and wall ahead, keeping an eye open for the presence of wild deer, which roam these uplands.

Head left along the main track as it swings north above Holme Wood and through a series of gates down to Kentmere Hall. The decay of the ancient pele tower is a stark reminder of a violent past in contrast to the white-washed charm of the abutting farm house. Bear right along the farm access track, which leads us directly back to the church and Kentmere village.

31. D IS FOR DODD

Start and Finish: Turn left up a side road past the pub in Dockray. Park on the grass verge after a half-mile, adjacent to a pair of barns at Green How.

Summits Climbed:	Clough Head	— 2381 feet
	Great Dodd	— 2807 feet
	Watson's Dodd	— 2584 feet
	Stybarrow Dodd	— 2770 feet
	Hart Side	— 2481 feet

Total Height Climbed: 2550 feet

Distance Walked: 11½ miles

Nearest Centre: Dockray

Map Required: Ordnance Survey English Lakes 1:25000, North East area sheet

INTRODUCTION

Stemming from the medieval meaning for a rounded hill, the Dodds present a more chastened image than their brash cousins to the south along the elongated spine, which centres upon the ever-popular Helvellyn. In consequence, fewer travellers pass this way and you are quite likely to have the tops to yourself. Short-tufted grass characterises the smoothly undulating surface of these giants, progress being swift and springy along the broad ridge.

The valley of Aira Beck encapsulates a landscape of abrupt contrasts that few others can rival. From the bleak swampy course of upper Deepdale, through one of the most serene mid-valley walks in Lakeland, it funnels down to the cataclysmic display of pure exhibitionism that is Aira Force. Few

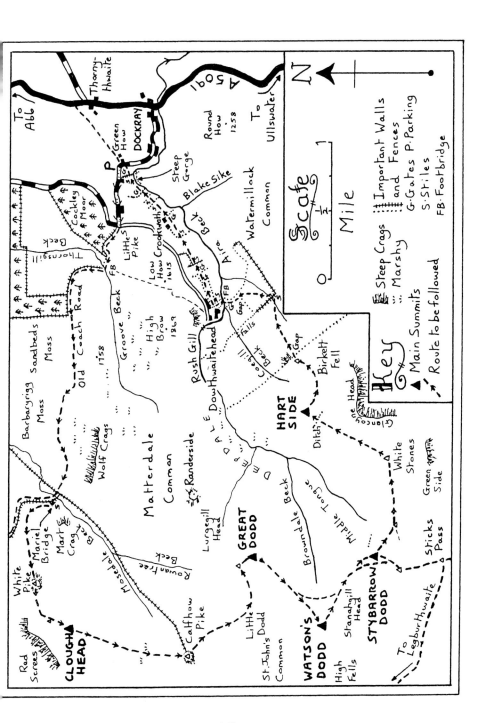

visitors stray far from this spectacle of raw savagery, which plummets down the enclosed wooded ravine to assist in swelling the girth of Ullswater.

Neither can anywhere else justifiably claim a greater affinity with the breed of sheep that has come to symbolise agrarian traditions in Lakeland. The built-in toughness of the white-faced Herdwick enables it to graze quite happily up to 3000 feet. An annual rainfall in excess of 200 inches is easily 'turned' by a thick hairy fleece, which is the cheapest on the market and used mainly in the manufacture of carpets and felting. Today the sheep are bred primarily for meat, the wool trade being slack and not very profitable after paying the shearers off.

Herdwicks possess an inherent loyalty to a particular heaf, which means that they are not prone to straying. It is not unknown for sheep to wander back to their native fell after having been sold to a farm in another area. Unlike their charges, however, local shepherds have adapted to a changing world by exchanging muscle power for that incorporated in the four-wheeled motorised fell buggy, which is a common sight nowadays, although sheep dogs do still perform their traditional herding duties.

ROUTE DESCRIPTION

Make your way in a westerly direction up the road from Green How until it turns sharp right at Cockley Moor forestry plantation. Continue ahead through a stile along the Old Coach Road, which follows a level course until its descent into St. John's-in-the-Vale. The way is straightforward as far as Mariel Bridge, a substantial structure over Mosedale Beck. The bleak surroundings must have witnessed the passing of much wheeled traffic in days gone by but I have never met anybody thus far.

Immediately beyond the bridge, cross a fence stile on your left and accompany the old road for a quarter of a mile before bearing left away up the grassy shoulder. Head due west towards the rocky tor of White Pike. A profusion of weathered boulders has made this a far more interesting summit than the undistinguished swathe of Clough Head itself. Keep to the edge of the abrupt downfall to Red Screes for the best scenery on the intervening half-mile to the summit.

Despite the presence of a trig column and shelter, there is little reason for tarrying overlong on Clough Head, so push on down the broad connecting plateau in a direct south-south-westerly line, making for Calfhow Pike. This half-way house between Clough Head and the first Dodd establishes an oasis of rock amidst the grassy moorland.

Clamber over the outcropping and continue south east to mount the gently graded slope over Little Dodd. Swing left up to the dual summit of Great Dodd. The first cairn is the main summit but a fine shelter 100 yards to the south east is the most sensible resting place for lunch. Thereafter, a simple south-westerly stroll will bring you to the barely discernible features of Watson's Dodd. From this angle it exhibits no mountain qualities at all and only impresses itself as a true fell when viewed from the west. A thin trail in the grass indicates that it is by-passed by the vast majority of travellers, who pass quickly on to the more acceptable form of Stybarrow Dodd. It is significant that the main path does not take you over the obvious summit for some inexplicable reason, so a deviation is necessary to rectify this omission.

The route to Hart Side is initially pathless. Head south east down the grassy flank of Stybarrow Dodd to join a thin trod at a distinctive cairn, thence continuing due east over White Stones. A wide sweep to the north culminates in a brief ascent onto Hart Side, once disparagingly referred to as Nameless Fell on past Ordnance Survey maps.

Make a wide left-hand swing, aiming for the distinguished cairn topping Birkett Fell. Immediately beyond, cross a broken wall to descend the tussocky slope into mid-Aira. Head north east for the in-take fence and a stile abutting a clear water course. Descend to the lower wall and follow it round to the extended settlement of Dowthwaitehead, where Aira Beck is crossed by a footbridge.

Turn left into a narrow walled lane, before bearing right to follow the north-east Matterdale path through the lower pastures. Make use of the large scale map overleaf for the rest of the walk. A series of stiles and gates allow passage along the one-and-a-half miles of this tranquil and largely unfrequented hanging valley. Local farmers are very friendly to those who have time to chat awhile and I passed an interesting half an hour chatting to a pair across the intervening boundary wall dividing their land.

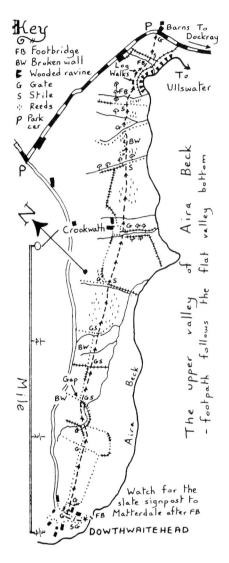

Key

FB Footbridge
BW Broken wall
▮ Wooded ravine
G Gate
S Stile
Reeds
P Park car

Barns To Dockray

Log Walks

To Ullswater

BW

Crookwath

N

Mile

The upper valley of Aira Beck - footpath follows the flat valley bottom

GS
BW
GS
Gap
BW
GS
G
G
FB
SG
DOWTHWAITEHEAD

Watch for the slate signpost to Matterdale after FB

The path bears right above the wooded slope where Aira Beck cuts through a steep gorge, before dropping down to Dockray and the more dramatic outburst that follows at the Force. A short stroll returns us to the barns of Green How and the culmination of a hike of some length, which introduces the lesser-known territory behind the grand façade of Ullswater.

152

32. THE ALTERNATIVE FAIRFIELD HORSESHOE

Start and Finish: Parking in Patterdale is strictly limited. Various roadside pull-ins are available of which the most reliable are at Bridgend a mile to the south of the village where there is never a problem.

Summits Climbed:	Arnison Crag	— 1424 feet
	Birks	— 2040 feet
	St Sunday Crag	— 2756 feet
	Fairfield	— 2863 feet

Total Height Climbed: 3200 feet

Distance Walked: 9½ miles

Nearest Centre: Patterdale

Map Required: Ordnance Survey English Lakes 1:25000, North East area sheet

INTRODUCTION

Every step of the renowned Fairfield Horseshoe has been followed religiously by countless pilgrims to such an extent that the apex of the route now resembles a cosmic no-man's-land. This alternative horseshoe hike offers a far more exhilarating circuit around the desolate Deepdale, visiting remote terrain where even the indigenous Herdwicks are in short supply.

Purists might well claim that any walk calling itself a horseshoe ought to descend the elongated ridge of Hartsop above How after crossing the bouldery confusion atop Hart Crag. Any walk that aims to transport its followers into

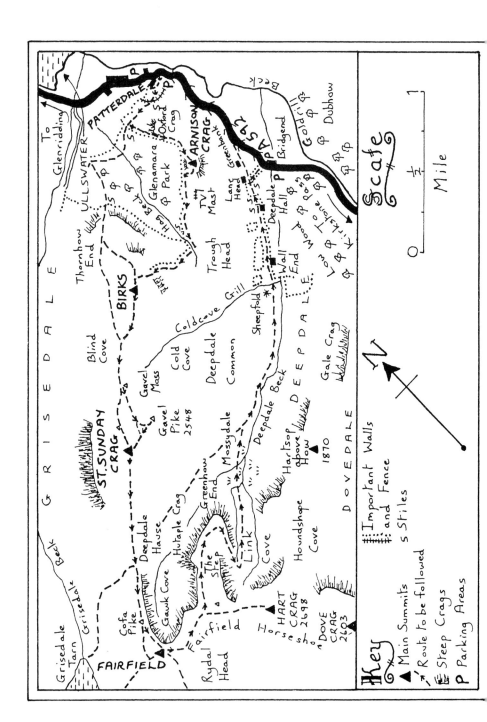

GRISEDALE

To Glenridding

PATTERDALE

ULLSWATER

Oxford Crag

Glenamara Park

ARNISON CRAG

TV Mast

A 592

Lang Head Greenbank

Bridgend

Goldrill

Dubhow

Beck

Deepdale Hall

Kirkstone

Wood

Wall End

Thornhow End

BIRKS

Trough Head

Blind Cove

Coldcove Gill

Deepdale Common

Sheepfold

Gavel Moss

Cold Cove

Gale Crag

Deepdale Beck

DEEPDALE

Gavel Pike 2548

ST. SUNDAY CRAG

Mossydale

Hartsop above How 1870

DOVEDALE

Deepdale Hause

Greenhow End

Link Cove

Houndshope Cove

Griesdale Beck

Hutaple Crag

The Step

Cofa Pike

Gawk Cove

Griesdale Tarn

FAIRFIELD

Rydal Head

Fairfield Horseshoe

HART CRAG 2698

DOVE CRAG 2603

Scale

0   ½   1

Mile

N

Key

▲ Main Summits
↗ Route to be followed
⋕⋕ Steep Crags
P Parking Areas

⫶⫶⫶ Important Walls and Fence
S Stiles

154

remote territory cannot do better than descend the elliptical arm of The Step into Link Cove. This pathless hanging valley remains a secluded backwater within the core of the Lake District. Such a rare phenomenon is to be savoured.

Originally regarded as a pre-eminent climbing ground with routes of over 400 feet, the savage buttresses of Hutaple and Scrubby Crags in Deepdale's upper recess have fallen out of favour in recent years. The fearsome reputation of Dovedale next door has attracted the cream of rock men like bees to a jampot. Nevertheless, to the lowly fellwalker, Fairfield presents an image of awe and mystery when viewed from the desolate wasteland below Greenhow End. This is a side of the mountain often overlooked, being hidden from those who fail to appreciate the intricate tapestry on its north face.

ROUTE DESCRIPTION

Immediately beyond the Patterdale lay-by, turn left up a rough track, past the hotel car park, then fork left along a side trail signposted to Grisedale. After a fence stile, the path climbs up by a wall, continuing ahead across Glenamara Park after the next stile. At this point, bear left up a steepening grass slope beside a wall, to pass beneath the overhanging branches of a well-seasoned horse chestnut.

Pressing on up the thin track, the climbers' practice wall of Oxford Crag comes into sight. Care is needed on its ascent. Keep with the wall until the gradient eases below the battlements of Arnison Crag. A short climb brings us onto the nobbly top, which provides a splendid northern aspect along Ullswater.

To rejoin the wall path, which encircles Glenamara Park, a sharp descent of the western rampart is necessary. At the valley head, cross over Hag Beck and begin the steep pull alongside a broken wall. This section is easy, but conversely is the most tiring section of the whole walk. Use the wall as a stairway to the heights above for a more stimulating ascent. When it terminates abruptly, continue ahead to join the ridge path coming up from Thornhow End, then head left onto the grass-clad summit of Birks.

There is little to encourage you to linger on the verdant dome, so maintain a south-westerly course to cross the Blind Cove col and mount the north-facing escarpment of St Sunday Crag. A prominent cairn marks the point where the path splits. Fork left to circle the bilberry couches that blanket the slopes above Gavel Moss. The next objective of Gavel Pike scores the horizon with its horny beak and is infinitely preferable as a lunch stop to the parent fell above.

A broad saddle connects with St Sunday Crag, which is soon attained after a brief uphill stroll. Head south west down the extended shoulder, crossing Deepdale Hause to scramble up the exciting arête beyond. As Cofa Pike is approached, the pitted blade narrows. The final tussle makes a fine ascent in its own right but is sadly dwarfed by the overpowering bulk of Fairfield.

Where the path bears right, a sporting alternative is to continue up the serrated rim onto the broad and somewhat confusing summit plateau ahead. However, Fairfield is not a place on which to wander in mist. The grass carpet has been worn away across much of the threadbare dome and is not an attractive spot to linger.

Join the wide track bearing south east around a gully, then east for a half-mile before swinging left down the scarred shoulder known as The Step. Beyond Hutaple Crag, the path narrows and slants right as the hidden drop of Greenhow End is approached. Make a hairpin right to descend the grass bank into Link Cove, then sharp left following a line of cairns. Care is needed to avoid slipping on the secluded rocks in the long grass. Few sheep make it into this lonely bastion to keep the lawn trimmed.

Make a steep descent on grass between the twin emergent streams, passing under the upthrust of Greenhow End. At valley level, cross the swampy morass of Mossydale to join the path descending from the Hause. Head north east down Deepdale, the path becoming a farm access road when the first walled settlement is reached. Stick with this until the third stile, after which a right takes us down a rough walled lane to the main road. A hundred yards to the left quickly returns us to the car pull-in.

33. ABOVE THE THWAITES OF BORROWDALE

Start and Finish: Numerous pull-ins are available along the Stone-thwaite road, a side turning that is signposted a half-mile south of Rosthwaite on the B5289.

Summits Climbed:

Bessyboot	— 1807 feet
Glaramara	— 2560 feet
Allen Crags	— 2572 feet
Seathwaite Fell	— 1970 feet

Total Height Climbed: 3000 feet

Distance Walked: 11½ miles

Nearest Centre: Stonethwaite

Maps Required: Ordnance Survey English Lakes 1:25000, North West and South West area sheets

---

INTRODUCTION

The head of Borrowdale provides some of the most spectacular scenery to be found in Lakeland. Carved from the scourging action of immense rivers of ice, the deep glacial troughs are understandably regarded with awe by the multitudes of fell wanderers who come to pay homage to the roof of England.

Seathwaite, a tiny farming hamlet at the valley head, is best avoided as a starting point, the access road being frequently choked with parked cars. Thankfully on my way back through the settlement, it failed to live up to its unenviable reputation as the wettest inhabited place in Britain. During the

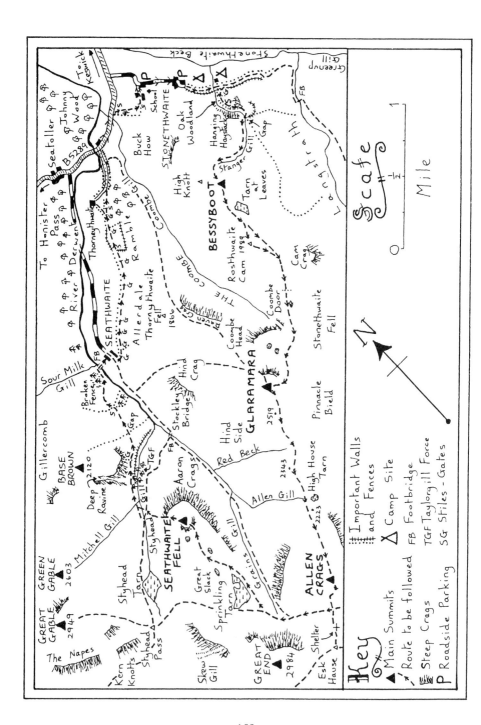

Key
Main Summits
Route to be followed
Steep Crags
P Roadside Parking

┼┼┼ Important Walls and Fences
△ Camp Site
FB Footbridge
TGF Taylorgill Force
SG Stiles - Gates

Scafe

0 — ½ — 1
Mile

N

last Ice Age, Seathwaite dipped its toes in the southern end of a temporary lake that has since drained away. Flooding, however, can still be a problem, the most recent inundation having occurred in 1966.

Beyond the bulky mass of Rosthwaite Fell lies Stonethwaite, which has so far managed to retain its ancient farming heritage. Originally a 13th-century 'vaccary', or dairy farm, the valley had to be cleared of its bouldery deposits by the monks before such agrarian enterprise could begin, a development which proved to be exceedingly profitable for the mother abbey at Fountains.

The word 'thwaite' appears with monotonous regularity hereabouts, testifying to the distinctive influence brought by colonising hordes of Norse settlers in the Middle Ages. This particular 'clearing' marks the commencement of a hike, the distance of which should not be underestimated. The way is long and somewhat confusing in its initial stages across the broad undulation of Rosthwaite Fell. Careful map reading is required over the intermittent paths and craggy outcrops, and it is most unlikely that fellow travellers will be encountered prior to attaining the summit of Glaramara.

ROUTE DESCRIPTION

Approaching Stonethwaite along the access road, the full splendour of the classic glaciated U-shaped valley becomes apparent. High on the steep right-hand flank, a distinctive cleft hewn from the rampart of Hanging Haystack provides a chink in the formidable armoury protecting Bessyboot.

After passing through the hamlet, take the rough lane that keeps slightly above the valley floor. This is the original route by which Cistercian monks transported wool and salt over Stake Pass. Haematite ore was also moved down to the iron smelter at the entrance to Langstrath, having been carried by pack horses over Ore Gap from the west coast.

After a quarter of a mile, pass through a gate to enter an open glade, before climbing through the lower slopes of oak woodland alongside Big Stanger Gill. Much of the old forest in this area was cut down by the Furness monks to provide charcoal for the iron bloomery in the valley. The way ahead is clear but becomes increasingly stony as height is gained. Beyond a wall stile, the deep gash of the ravine can be fully appreciated. (A friend assures me that Stanger Gill makes an exciting gorge scramble for those of a more ebullient persuasion.) Looking north, mid-Borrowdale lies resplendent under a verdant patchwork quilt, stitched with grey stone walling and secured by the pincer jaws of Castle Crag and Kings How.

Emerging from the confines of the ravine, follow the gill to the right over a broken wall end in a westerly direction. On a first visit, the undefined nature of scattered outcroppings may seem a trifle perplexing. Re-cross the gill where an obvious cairn is seen perched on a boulder ahead. Make your way around the edge of a marshy arena to approach Bessyboot from the north. Viewed from the summit, Tarn at Leaves can be seen nestling cosily on a grass couch to the south.

Our way passes to the right, following an easy trail towards the strking rock plinth of Rosthwaite Cam, the highest point on the ridge, which can be visited if time permits. When the path fades, try to maintain a south-south-westerly course across the series of swampy depressions, each protected by abrupt craggy fortifications. The final redoubt is breached across a spongy plain, prior to bearing left to approach Glaramara up a gradually ascending causeway.

The rock-strewn summit makes a good spot for lunch, with superb views of Skiddaw to the north. The only easy exit lies south south west along the roller-coaster ridge to Allen Crags. Meandering across an ever-changing landscape with mountain pools enclosed in a series of depressions, the delightful path should present no difficulties in any weather.

Beyond Allen Crags, a short descent brings you close to the celebrated pass of Esk Hause. The pass proper lies a quarter of a mile south west and 100 feet higher at the head of Upper Eskdale. In mist this lower col can easily lead to errors that direct the unwary in a completely false direction. So, beware and do not stray beyond the cross wall shelter, which is a favoured grub stop made use of by those bound for the 'Roof'.

Make a right here and follow a clear track down towards Sprinkling Tarn under the towering buttress of Great End. Even during the height of summer, the absence of prolonged sun ensures the presence of snow tails trapped within the soaring gullies. After the eroded defile of Grains Gill veers to the north, fork right off the main path to pass Sprinkling Tarn on your left. Maintain a northerly course on the hummocky approach to the summit of Seathwaite Fell, which rises little above the bleak surroundings.

Not another living creature was encountered. Perhaps this upland lies under the spell of local 'boggles' who resent any intrusion into their domain. If you harbour a superstitious nature, maybe Seathwaite Fell should be avoided. From the final rock platform sporting a substantial cairn, those of us who cock a nonchalant snook at spectral residents should head due west down an increasingly steep slope.

Cross the main path from Sty Head to join a less-frequented alternative on the far bank. Head north east along a narrow trail, which entails some simple scrambling under the east face of Base Brown. The impressive cataract of Taylorgill Force lies to your right.

Bear left out of the confines of the lower section of Styhead Gill to follow a distinct path down to Seathwaite. A footbridge across the infant Derwent gives access to the hamlet down a walled lane. Bear right under the farm archway to locate a signpost pointing the way left through the first of numerous gates. This is the start of the Allerdale Ramble, one of various long-distance routes that have sprung up in the Lake District.

Upon reaching the main valley road, head right for a quarter of a mile until the B5289 crosses Coombe Gill. A gate on the right gives access to a farm track across the fields, passing the old church of St Andrews prior to rejoining Stonethwaite Lane. In early spring, the colourful exhibition of daffodils scattered across the well-kept graveyard does much to dispel the unwarranted myth that such places must always be sombre and mournful.

34. MYSTERIES OF MUNGRISDALE

Start and Finish: Ample parking space is available on the wide grass verge opposite the green village hall in Mungrisdale.

Summits Climbed:	Souther Fell	— 1680 feet
	Blencathra	— 2847 feet
	Bowscale Fell	— 2306 feet

Total Height Climbed: 2850 feet

Distance Walked: 9 miles

Nearest Centre: Mungrisdale

Map Required: Ordnance Survey Landranger 90 1:50000, Penrith, Keswick and Ambleside area

---

INTRODUCTION

Many are the stories that have been handed down through generations regarding the appearance of ghosts and strange apparitions in the Lake District. Yet none has been more authenticated than that told of the spectral army of Souther Fell. The first sighting was in 1735 by two farmworkers, who witnessed a column of marching soldiers that lasted for a full hour. In later years, numerous sightings were made by local citizenry, but no footprints were ever found anywhere on Souther Fell.

It has been suggested that this was a form of mirage depicting real Jacobite troops on manoeuvres to the north. Perhaps this is true since no further sightings have been reported over the last 200 years. The only travellers likely to be seen on Souther Fell these days will be spectral images of those scurrying up the ice-carved ridges of Blencathra.

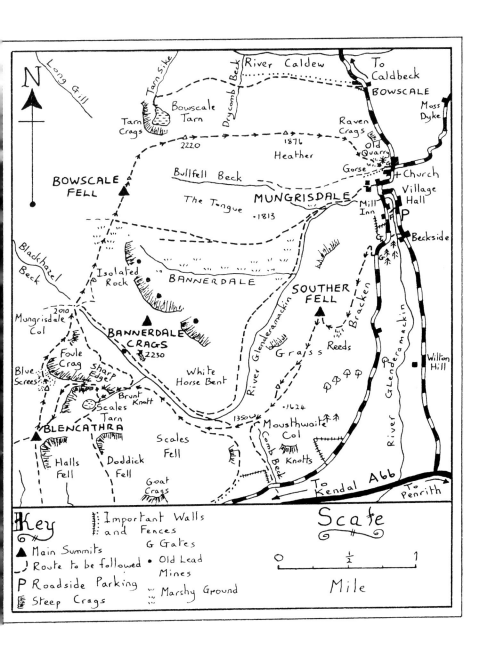

Key

- ▲ Main Summits
- ⌣ Route to be followed
- P Roadside Parking
- ⛰ Steep Crags
- ⫴ Important Walls and Fences
- G Gates
- • Old Lead Mines
- ⸪ Marshy Ground

Scale

0 — ½ — 1

Mile

Map labels:

Long Grill
River Caldew
To Caldbeck
BOWSCALE
Moss Dyke
Tarn Sike
Bowscale Tarn
Drycomb Beck
Tarn Crags
Raven Crags
Old Quarry
△2220
Heather
1876
Church
BOWSCALE FELL
Gorse
Village Hall
Bullfell Beck
MUNGRISDALE
The Tongue
•1813
Mill Inn
P
Beckside
Blackhazel Beck
Isolated Rock
BANNERDALE
SOUTHER FELL
G
Mungrisdale Col
2010
River Glenderamackin
Grass Reeds
Bracken
BANNERDALE CRAGS
2230
Foule Crag
White Horse Bent
Wilton Hill
Blue Screes
Sharp Edge
Brunt Knott
Scales Tarn
•1624
River Glenderamackin
BLENCATHRA
1350
Mousthwaite Col
Halls Fell
Scales Fell
Doddick Fell
Comb Beck
Knotts
Goat Crags
To Kendal A66
To Penrith

Approached from the south, Blencathra presents an appearance akin to some primitive creature awaiting its unsuspecting prey. Grasping talons reach out to ensnare unwitting mortals who dare to trespass upon its domain. Care and concentration are required on its ascent.

Prepare, therefore, to enter a new dimension, remote and mysterious, an outpost of the imagination where all things are possible.

ROUTE DESCRIPTION

Opposite the village hall where you have parked, make use of a footbridge over the River Glenderamackin, which provides access to the Mill Inn. Do not, however, be tempted at such an early hour. Instead, turn away left down the narrow lane. After passing through a gate, continue ahead for no more than 200 yards, watching for a distinct track cutting back up the bracken-clad slope on the right.

Take this track, which soon wheels to the left slanting uphill across the eastern flank of Souther Fell. The path follows a grass shelf, climbing steadily above the upper limit of the bracken cloak. Still on grass, continue ahead as far as a distinct clump of reeds blocking further progress. At this point, strike up the pathless grass slope in a wide arc bearing right, which should bring you to the summit.

A strange feature relating to Souther Fell is that it boasts all the characteristics of a coastal peninsula. Instead of dipping its toes in the Irish Sea, however, in this case it is the Glenderamackin. Draining from the upper slopes of Bannerdale Crags, the river is thwarted from a direct link with the westbound Greta by the shallow obstruction known as Mousthwaite Col. Instead, it slips north to circumvent Souther Fell, cutting an agressive sway through Mungrisdale before isolating the noble upthrust.

From the summit, head south west across a shallow depression, taking a right fork to visit a far more statuesque edifice overlooking the Glenderamackin Valley and Bannerdale Crags opposite. Rejoin the main path and descend easy grass slopes to cross Mousthwaite Col. Merge with the upcoming path from Scales and head north-west into the confines of the upper valley.

Focus ahead on the ragged fangs of Sharp Edge backed by the exposed cliff that is Foule Crag. The mile-long stroll provides ample time to prepare yourself for this epic challenge.

Where Scales Beck cuts a deep channel through to coalesce with the Glenderamackin, the decision has to be made as to what excuses need to be invented for evading the Sharp Edge ascent. If a pressing appointment with your accountant is suddenly brought to mind, cross the beck to follow a thin trail up to the head of the valley and Mungrisdale Col. Superheroes strike up the beck, soon crossing to the north bank and ascending the narrow gorge under Brunt Knott.

Scales Tarn is a hidden gem, a perfect corrie neatly tucked away out of sight behind the grand façade. But rumour has it that the tarn is bottomless and so completely devoid of the sun's warmth that at midday, a reflection of the stars might be espied glistening on its sable waters. Bear right immediately before the tarn up an easy grass-covered banking with the Edge ahead. Although a path lurks below the north face, stick to the saw-toothed rim for the best sport.

Take heed of the acutely broken nature of the ribbed blade. Sharp Edge is indeed well named. At the terminus of the arête, the precipice of Foule Crag must be climbed. It may be that the sight of this denizen strikes fear into those of a nervous disposition, but many holds turn this into an exhilarating scramble for the adventurous. As the gradient eases, follow a clear path around the upper ledge of the corrie and so to the famed summit, where an unforgettable panorama of mountain Lakeland is laid out in all its majestic splendour.

Poised on the brink of the beast's prominent snout, this is no place for the faint-hearted or those prone to vertigo. Head due north across the 'saddle-back' that gives the mountain its alternative name to enjoy lunch by a large cairn overlooking Foule Crag. A path zig-zags down Blue Screes, after which an easy stroll on grass down the north ridge brings us to Mungrisdale Col.

Go straight across bearing half left on a thin trail that points a finger towards Bowscale Fell. Beyond a conspicuous boulder, all is grass. Midway, a marshy tract has to be negotiated but poses no difficulties to the final objective directly ahead a quarter of a mile away. The stony summit of Bowscale Fell

. is marked by a rock shelter. Make your way past a subsidiary cairn 100 yards to the north east, after which a wide loop to the right brings us to the east ridge. Mount a stony rise to a nameless top where Bowscale Tarn can be seen 500 feet below. A pair of trout might be observed cavorting in the placid waters, as noted by Wordsworth in his 'Feast of Brigham Castle'.

A gentle descent along the ridge, pathless at first, is a delightful finale to this spell-binding hike. The walking is easy with little loss of height until the last quarter of a mile when the path drops steeply through a protective shield of gorse. Below this, a grass bank to the right of an old quarry brings us out onto the road north of Mungrisdale village.

Take a right here along the road for a half-mile passing St Kentigern's Church and so back to our starting point.

35. CRINKLE CRUNCHING

Start and Finish: The open road on either side of Cockley Beck Bridge provides ample roadside parking space.

Summits Climbed:	Crinkle Crags	— 2816 feet
	Little Stand	— 2405 feet
Total Height Climbed:	2250 feet	
Distance Walked:	6 miles	
Nearest Centre:	Boot, Eskdale	
Map Required:	Ordnance Survey English Lakes 1:25000, South West area sheet	

INTRODUCTION

After motoring north up the meandering wooded enclave that encompasses the Duddon Valley, the landscape suddenly opens up as you reach the lowland centred on Cockley Beck. Comprising no more than a single building, the bridge is a meeting of roads — a route focus to the cognoscenti.

Here, the only road gate in the district forces vehicles to open and close this continuation of the farm boundary fence. It has always struck me as strange that no larger settlement ever developed on this site. Perhaps, lying deep within the mountain fastness, it was too remote for even the hardy Norse settlers to contemplate.

Cockley Beck provides a stepping stone to another highway that radiates from the junction, the unfrequented Mosedale Valley. In old Norse, the name means 'valley of the bog', an aptly fitting title in its middle reaches.

167

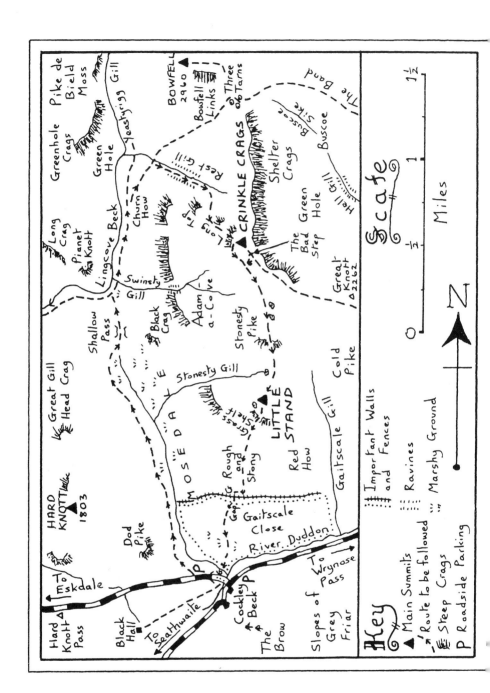

ROUTE DESCRIPTION

Follow the clear trail that forks right off the road beyond Cockley Beck Bridge, and head north-north-west on the left bank of Mosedale Beck. Passing below the gnarled outcropping of Dod Pike, the solid route cuts a swathe through the bracken. The first mile remains dry underfoot and makes for pleasant walking.

As the way becomes more swampy underfoot, abandon the original track to follow a higher level trod above the worst of the bog. Swinging round to the right, make a gradual ascent to cross a shallow pass.

A brief descent on grass finds us merging with the track alongside Lingcove Beck, coming up from Eskdale. Bear right to pursue a delightful course towards the towering pyramid of Bowfell, which dominates the valley head. The track soon begins to climb, initially on grass, to the right of Churn How. As height is gained, watch for the gorge carved out by the surging might of Rest Gill, flowing beneath the bed rocks in its lower reaches.

At this point, decide whether you prefer to continue ahead to Three Tarns, and then along the roller coaster ridge of the Crinkles, an easier but longer route, or to snatch up the gauntlet of the infinitely more challenging and preferable conquest of the principal summit by way of this awesome ravine. The choice is yours. I opted for the latter, preferring the opportunity for an exhilarating gorge scramble, steeply rocky and hemmed in with not a soul in sight.

Keep in the bed of Rest Gill as much as possible for the best scrambling. Where this becomes difficult, escape up the bilberry slope on the right provides an easy alternative. When the gradient eases, bear right away from the gill to gain the broad craggy shoulder of Long Top. A series of broken elbows, pathless but following a south-easterly bearing, brings us to the loftiest of the five individual tops collectively known as Crinkle Crags.

The rough nature of the ridge is abruptly announced when continuing down a cataclysmic rent in the rock wall. The Bad Step is easily avoided but adds a spicy piquancy to the main course and should not be shunned. Nonetheless, care and respect for every facet of mountain terrain must be automatic for all fell wanderers.

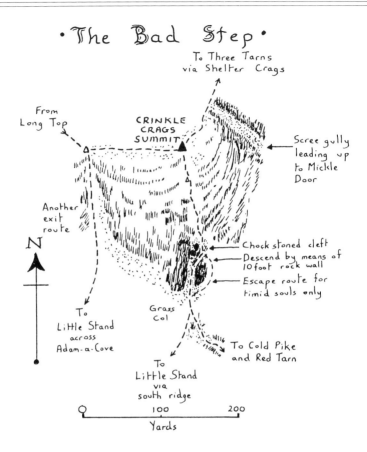

· The Bad Step ·

To Three Tarns
via Shelter Crags

From
Long Top

CRINKLE
CRAGS
SUMMIT

Scree gully
leading up
to Mickle
Door

Another
exit
route

N

Chock stoned cleft
Descend by means of
10 foot rock wall

Escape route for
timid souls only

To
Little Stand
across
Adam-a-Cove

Grass
Col

To Cold Pike
and Red Tarn

To
Little Stand
via
south ridge

0   100   200

Yards

There are few if any impassable sections for walkers negotiating ridge trails in Lakeland. Progress down this awesome cleft in the south face of the summit tower is barred by a pair of balancing chockstones. Easy to avoid by returning west to a prominent cairn and thence south down a loose rake, this must surely be a cop-out for intrepid explorers used to living on the wild side. As the eroded path steepens, aim to the right, soon arriving at the lip of a ten-foot rock wall below the chocks. Too far to jump, it will require careful selection of strategically-placed holds if sprained ankles are to be avoided.

At the base of the col below the Bad Step, head right to circumvent the final crinkle and so gain the south ridge. Look for a thin trail that contours the west flank, prior to negotiating the rock-encrusted knuckle of Stonesty Pike.

Continue south across a grassy depression and up onto the gnarled ridge culmination of Little Stand. Left of the summit, the path descends through a gap in the upper ramparts. Beyond a broad grass shelf, the final slope is reached. Here the path disappears amid a welter of boulders whose sole purpose is to trap the unwary. Rest a while before making the arduous downfall. In the distance what appear to be dinky toys can be seen snaking up Hard Knott Pass.

Eventually, the muscle-jarring descent will have to be faced. Take it easy and pick your own careful passage between the chaotic rash down to the in-take fence. Follow it west as far as a gate. Pass through this and the old wall gap to cross Gaitscale Close, and head back to Cockley Beck on a well-used farm track.

This is a testing circuit for the adventurous fell hound and is not recommended in poor conditions, due to the distinctly rough terrain and an absence of paths.

36. EAST OF THE DUDDON

Start and Finish: A small car park by the local church at Seathwaite provides ample space.

Summits Climbed:		
	Caw	— 1735 feet
	Pikes	— 1520 feet
	White Pike	— 1943 feet
	White Maiden	— 1976 feet
	Brown Pike	— 2239 feet
	Dow Crag	— 2555 feet

Total Height Climbed: 2850 feet

Distance Walked: 10 miles

Nearest Centre: Ulpha

Map Required: Ordnance Survey English Lakes 1:25000, South West area sheet

INTRODUCTION

No experience on earth can quite surpass that of being a lone walker in fell country where Man's impact on the landscape has long since blended into the pages of history. This is especially so when the expansive panorama on view from one's very own corner of heaven is honed to an image of crystal clarity. Cold sun-dappled winter days when below-zero temperatures have frozen the underlying substratum are a joy to savour, but not to linger over as days are short and the crisp ozone quickly chills one to the bone.

The delectable fell country east of the Duddon is particularly pleasing in this respect. Tracks are few and those that do slice the terrain are long and well made, having been laid down for the use of miners and travellers. The Walna

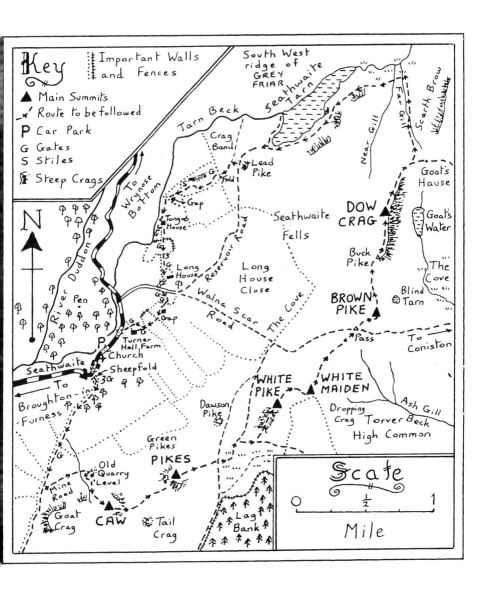

Scar Road is the most notable, providing a cross-fell route between Seathwaite and Coniston, the pass of which is the fifth highest in Lakeland.

Less attention has been paid to the Duddon Valley than to other more eminent dales, not because it is any less attractive — far from it. But it certainly is different, having no lake and assuming a more tortuous orientation than the classic glacial mould. The river and attendant becks babble and chatter between craggy spurs in a sylvan enclave, where natural woodland complements the surging ranks of conifer plantings that have taken over much of the west flank.

Dunnerdale will never become another Langdale. Lying tucked away in the less accessible south-west corner of the Lake District, it will always remain the territory of the connoisseur who prefers his own company.

ROUTE DESCRIPTION

From the church, walk south down the road towards a sharp right turn at the Newfield Inn. There is plenty of parking space in the hamlet but only for those prepared to make good use of their right arm. Those of us exercising the feet should make a left here, passing through a sheep pen with three gates. Follow the wall round to the right and stick with it through the oak woodland.

Climb steadily out of the valley on a clear track called Park Head Road. After passing through a wall gate, watch for a sharp left that slants across the fell on a well-constructed causeway bound for the old quarry. As the spoil tips are approached, the trail makes a zig-zag up to a flooded mine level. A further zig-zag leads you ever up the steepening fellside, where a faintly discernible cairned path follows beside a stream. At its source, pursue a south-easterly bearing, towards Caw's trig column, which is visible from below.

The summit is a splendid rocky plinth, which falls away rapidly establishing a mountain form in miniature that is clearly recognisable from across Morecambe Bay. The name Caw comes from the Norse word for calf. The northern prospect across Dunnerdale is dominated by an arresting skyline fronted by the Scafells.

Take a course east-north-east across the intervening depression toward Pikes a half-mile distant. Avoid the red herring offered by Tail Crag, a thumb of splintered rock that had me fooled initially. Even in superb conditions where paths are in short supply, the compass shouldn't be left pocketed.

Continue down to another major track, taking the right fork around Caw Moss. At this point, the towering rampart of White Pike might appear a somewhat daunting prospect, but it does provide first-rate scrambling to the apex of this under-rated top. The twin peak of White Maiden is soon gained thereafter across a shallow col, followed by a high-level stroll along Walna Scar ridge to the pass.

From here over Brown Pike and Buck Pike, the well-utilised path indicates the popularity of this section. One is likely to encounter a continuous stream of hikers en route for Dow Crag, a magnificent and uncompromising roost overlooking the scooped hollow of Goat's Water, 1000 feet below.

After dropping down to Goat's Hause, head left away from the crowds and follow a youthful Far Gill into the remote amphitheatre of Upper Tarn Beck. Watch out for a thin cairned path, which will lead you south east along a delightfully sinuous trail around the back of Shudderstone How and down to the water's edge. Make your way along to the southern end where a dam controls the outflow.

Unlike the major water supply schemes that have caused irreversible changes in their valleys, such as those at Thirlmere and Haweswater, this tarn is a small reservoir under the control of the Barrow authority. Apart from the dam and access road, there are thankfully no unsightly intrusions into the landscape nor disruptive elements affecting the valley communities. It is to be hoped that in these times of rapidly increasing water usage, future attempts to extract this vital resource in the Lake District will be planned with minimum impact.

Continue down the reservoir road for a third of a mile. Opposite Lead Pike, join a grass path to swing right through a walled gate and down the rough bank of Tongue House Close.

The valley route back to Seathwaite passes through the farmyard of Tongue House, thence through a pair of gates and across the fields to Long

House. Cross over the metalled access road to Walna Scar and through another field behind an old farm with modern annex. The clear track leads us back to the main valley road past Turner Hall Farm where a left turn will bring you back to the car park. This is a long walk across largely unfrequented terrain and all the more enjoyable for that. Enjoy it on a clear day to gain the full benefit.

37. SCAFELL PIKE — THE MOUNTAINS' MOUNTAIN

Start and Finish: 300 yards south of the Wasdale Head Inn, an open grass tract on the right of the road provides ample parking space.

Summits Climbed:	Scafell Pike	— 3210 feet
	Lingmell	— 2649 feet

Total Height Climbed: 3300 feet

Distance Walked: 7½ miles

Nearest Centre: Wasdale Head

Map Required: Ordnance Survey English Lakes 1:25000, South West area sheet

INTRODUCTION

'. . . round the top of Scawfell-Pike not a
blade of grass is to be seen. Cushions
or tufts of moss, parched and brown,
appear between the huge blocks and stones
that lie in heaps on all sides to a great
distance, like skeletons or bones of the
earth not needed at the creation, and
there left to be covered with never dying
lichens, which the clouds and dews nourish.'

Wordsworth's lyrical description of the roof of England visited in the autumn of 1810 is equally appropriate today. He might well, however, have had some choice epithet to pronounce on the nuclear intrusion so prominent on the

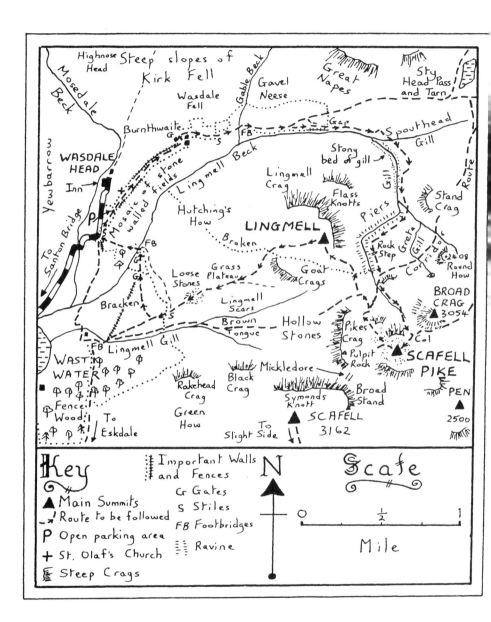

Highnose Head · Steep slopes of Kirk Fell

Mosedale Beck

Gable Beck

Gavel Neese

Great Napes

Sty Head Pass and Tarn

Wasdale Fell

Burnthwaite

FB

Gap

Spouthead Gill

Yewbarrow

WASDALE HEAD

Inn

Lingmell Beck

Stony bed of gill

Gill

Route

P

Mosaic of stone walled fields

Lingmell Crag

Flass Knotts

Piers

Stand Crag

To Santon Bridge

Hutching's How

LINGMELL

Greta Gill

FB

Broken

Rock Step

2408 Round How

Loose Stones

Grass Plateau

Goat Crags

Col

Bracken

Lingmell Scars

BROAD CRAG 3054

S

Brown Tongue

Hollow Stones

Pikes Crag

Col

FB Lingmell Gill

Pulpit Rock

SCAFELL PIKE

WAST WATER

Mickledore

Broad Stand

PEN

Rakehead Crag

Black Crag

Symonds Knott

2500

Fence Wood

Green How

SCAFELL 3162

To Eskdale

To Slight Side

Key

Main Summits

Route to be followed

P Open parking area

+ St. Olaf's Church

Steep Crags

Important Walls and Fences

G Gates

S Stiles

FB Footbridges

Ravine

N

Scale

0   ½   1

Mile

178

west coast at Sellafield. Almost two centuries of continuous visitation have witnessed scarring by major paths scratched white by the passage of a million boots aiming for the 'Stone Man', a topper of monumental proportions in contrast to the original solitary pole erected by the Ordnance Survey.

The honour of being England's crowning glory means that Scafell Pike (old Norse for bare fell) has become the mecca for a myriad of pilgrims, all anxious to notch up the mightiest of the 3000-footers. Yet barely a handful bother to deviate from the hallowed trail to visit the attendant guardians of which Broad Crag is probably the roughest and most cragfast in Lakeland.

Savage indeed is the Pike when tackled head on. But only when viewed from afar can its true majestic form be appreciated and then as part of an integrated whole. The Pike itself is merely the apex of a two-and-a-half mile ridge system stretching from Slight Side (2499 feet) to Great End (2984 feet).

Only crag hoppers and foot sloggers tread these wild and savage ramparts. No quiet pastures here for the indigenous Herdwick to nibble. Remote from inhabited settlements, this bone-crunching rock garden is not for the squeamish. Renowned as the wettest point in the Lake District, it can also be the most ferocious in winter, being one of the last summits to shed its icy cloak. Even in bright sunshine one December morn, the intense cold saw fit to freeze my army surplus water bottle rock solid. With its massive tiers of brutal rock, Scafell Pike issues the ultimate challenge, stark and bold with no concession to those seeking an easy ascent.

Wasdale furnishes the most spectacular of valley heads. It is little wonder, therefore, that the National Park has adopted the north-east prospect up the valley for its logo. Great Gable holds centre stage with the supporting cast of Yewbarrow and Lingmell introducing a production of mammoth proportions. And concealed in the wings, our star performer awaits his final curtain call cosseted by doting minions. Approaching Wasdale Head, the curtain rises to reveal this truly magnificent spectacle in all its glory.

ROUTE DESCRIPTION

From the car park, follow the wall on your right into a rough lane, passing the smallest parish church in the country on the left. Either side of the lane reveals an irregular mosaic of tiny walled fields, which have evolved to give a distinctive feel to the landscape of Wasdale Head. In the 18th-century when common land was enclosed, huge 'clearance cairns' were erected from surplus stones removed from the pastures. The end of the lane opens into the farmyard of Burnthwaite. Bear left through a gate, then right behind the buildings.

Continue up the valley under the dominating presence of Great Gable. After a wall stile, the track crosses Gable Beck by means of a footbridge. Two hundred yards further, watch for an indistinct right fork off the main track. It sticks close to the side of Lingmell Beck whilst the Styhead route climbs steadily across Gable's scree-choked south face towards the pass.

At the upper end of the last in-take wall, pass through a gap and follow a thin trail alongside the beck, crossing at the confluence of Spouthead Gill and Piers Gill. An enjoyable series of zig-zags ascends the tongue between the two. Resist the temptation to take a direct route. Nothing is more annoying than the unnecesary destruction of long-established zig-zag routes. When these end, slant across right to the edge of Piers Gill.

Climb steadily alongside the wide rock bed up to its junction with Greta Gill. The view south west up the deep gash of Piers Gill is breathtaking. From this point up to the head of the ravine, there is no safe means of crossing to the opposite bank. All around, stunning cliffs of splintered crag present an apparently insurmountable frontage. Yet all is not lost. An interesting route picks its way up the side of the ravine after crossing Greta Gill.

As the upper dogleg is neared, take advantage of the exhilarating scramble up a 50-foot rock step, before veering right to rejoin the gaping void above. In 1921, one of the hottest and driest Julys on record, witnessed the rescue of a barely conscious hiker who had lain injured in the bed of the upper gill for 20 days. Rescue teams had abandoned the search and his discovery by a group of climbers descending the gill proved to be an extremely fortuitous coincidence.

Beyond Middleboot Knotts, the gradient eases towards the end of the ravine and a simple stroll on grass brings us to the corridor route, the principal approach to Scafell Pike from Styhead Pass. Bear right to the termination of the ravine, then strike left up a gentle slope beside the stream to its source.

A steepening gully composed of loose scree brings us to Broad Crag Col. Those with kryptonite in their veins and fire in their belly might consider the scrambling ascent of Broad Crag direct from the corridor, making use of easy-angled rock slabs. The mountain above is a riotous confusion of substantial boulders, and great care is needed if ankle bones are to remain intact.

From the col, take a right up the heavily-eroded north-east face of the Pike to gain the hikers' mecca. The well-built plinth, set amidst a heaving swell of grey surf, remains a magnet for all fell walkers. The small map gives some idea of the paths radiating from the top. To descend, our way lies north west along a boot-scarred trail, which pursues a tortuous course down to Lingmell Col.

Cross the old wall, now much disintegrated, and ascend the opposite slope onto the summit of Lingmell, which sports a regal crown six feet in height overlooking the abrupt downfall into Piers Gill. Across the gulf occupied by Lingmell Beck, Gable, not wishing to be upstaged by its loftier neighbour, issues an unmistakable challenge for another day.

Head west from the summit rocks down a gently-shelving pathless grass slope, aiming to the right of Goat Crags ahead. Cross the old wall, bearing south west over a grass plateau, to merge with a clear path slanting down from Goat Crags. The steep descent of the west shoulder is unexpected and initially very loose, and requires care. Loss of almost a 1000 feet is rapid up to the in-take wall, where a stile is crossed.

Continue down a grass causeway, keeping a watchful eye open for a crossroads in the bracken. Take a right here to slant down an easy gradient between scattered trees. Beyond a wall gate, cross a small field through another gate to gain the opposite bank of Lingmell Beck using a foot bridge. Thereafter, a pleasant stroll across lowland pastures through a swathe of gorse brings us to the valley access road. Turn north for 100 yards back to the car park.

Any ascent of the mountains' mountain must entail a considerable degree of sweat and strain. But the opportunity of setting foot within such a fearsome arena of rock savagery ensures a memorable experience that any fell wanderer ought positively to embrace with gusto.